Meditating on the Word

MEDITATING ON THE WORD

DIETRICH BONHOEFFER

*Translated and Edited
by David McI. Gracie*

A COWLEY PUBLICATIONS BOOK

Lanham, Chicago, New York, Toronto, and Plymouth, UK

A COWLEY PUBLICATIONS BOOK

ROWMAN & LITTLEFIELD PUBLISHERS, INC.

Published in the United States of America
by Rowman & Littlefield Publishers, Inc.
A wholly owned subsidiary of The Rowman & Littlefield Publishing Group, Inc.
4501 Forbes Boulevard, Suite 200, Lanham, Maryland 20706
www.rowmanlittlefield.com

Estover Road
Plymouth PL6 7PY
United Kingdom

British Library Cataloguing in Publication Information Available

Library of Congress Cataloging-in-Publication Data

Bonhoeffer, Dietrich, 1906–1945.
[Selections. English. 2000]
    Meditating on the Word / Dietrich Bonhoeffer; translated by
    David Gracie. —2nd ed.
    p. cm.
    Includes bibliographical references.
    I. Meditation—Christianity 2. Sermons, German—
    Translations into English. 3. Bible. O.T. Psalms—Sermons.
    4. Bible. O.T. Psalms—Meditations. 5. Bekennende Kirche—
    Sermons. 6. United churches—Germany—Sermons.
    I. Gracie, David McI., 1932– II. Title.
    BV4813 .B62313 2000
    248—dc21   00-055488
    ISBN-13: 978-1-56101-184-1 (pbk. : alk. paper)
    ISBN-10: 1-56101-184-3 (pbk. : alk. paper)
Printed in the United States of America.

⊖™ The paper used in this publication meets the minimum requirements of
American National Standard for Information Sciences—Permanence of
Paper for Printed Library Materials, ANSI/NISO Z39.48-1992.

CONTENTS

✳

INTRODUCTION

Our Need for God's Word

"Your word is a lantern to my feet," says the psalmist, "and a light upon my path" (119:105). For many, however, the Bible is only a closed book on a shelf or a book to be opened as a literary and historical curiosity. But in Christianity, the religion of the Incarnate Word, what keeps bringing the word alive for us is the witness of those men and women who have been hearers and doers of the word. Pastor Dietrich Bonhoeffer is certainly one of those witnesses. These meditations of his on the words of Scripture may enable us to allow the light of the word to shine on our paths.

Much ink has been used in the debates over the centuries about the "inspiration" of Holy Scripture. Just how holy is it, and who made it so? But I like best the aphorism of the Jewish philosopher who said, "Inspiration is measured by what it has inspired." That philosopher is Emmanuel Levinas, a teacher of the word himself, whose understanding of the commandments of God as leading to a life lived for others is like that of Bonhoeffer's, a Lutheran pastor who preached Christ as "the man for others."

On April 9, 1945, before he was taken away to be executed by the Nazis after being implicated in the plot to kill Adolf Hitler, Bonhoeffer led a prayer service for the other prisoners who were with him. Among the texts for that Sunday on which he commented was Isaiah 53:5, "By his stripes we are healed." He taught the meaning of that passage by his own death, which has become a source of healing for subsequent generations of Christians who have tried to come to terms with their church's role in the persecution and slaughter of the Jews of Europe.

"He paid for God's Word with his life and taught God's Word by his death." This epitaph is from a novel that Bonhoeffer was writing in prison, and it applies very much to the author himself. In the same novel he has a woman leaving a Sunday service deeply dissatisfied by the sermon she has just heard. She reflects on the situation in Germany where the preaching and teaching of the Word seem to be dying out:

> The congregation, the entire locality, her own family were left without the Word of God and that meant that sooner or later their life must become completely disoriented. . . . Was it God's will to judge this generation by withdrawing his Word from them? But even if this was so . . . God wanted people who would oppose this judgment, who by God's Word would hold fast to him and not let go until he blessed them.[1]

Holding fast by means of God's word, Bonhoeffer spoke out early and publicly against Nazism and on behalf of the Jews, saying that "the church has an unconditional obligation to the victims of any ordering of society." In 1939 he left the temporary security of Union Theological Seminary in New York City to go home to Germany and head an underground seminary of the Confessing Church. This was the breakaway communion of those who separated themselves from the national church that followed Hitler. Later he joined in the active opposition to Hitler while serving in a military intelligence unit. The story is well known and needs no retelling here. What deserves our closer attention is how his story and the biblical story merged, how he came to live, as one of his greatest admirers, William Stringfellow, put it, "in a continuing biblical context."

The night of November 7-8, 1938, the night that has become known as *Kristallnacht,* in cities across Germany Jews were attacked and killed, their synagogues and businesses ransacked and burned. Joseph Goebbels, Hitler's minister of propaganda, wrote in his diary, "As I drive back to my hotel I hear the shop window glass smashing. Bravo! Bravo! The synagogues burn like big old shacks."

Bonhoeffer's friend and biographer, Eberhard Bethge, tells us how Bonhoeffer's Bible became his diary for *Kristallnacht.* In the Bible that he used for his daily meditations, the date 9-11-38 is written in the margin of Psalm 74, at verse 7, "They said to themselves, 'Let us destroy them altogether.' They burned down all the meeting places of God in the land." The following verse is underlined, with an exclamation point in the margin: "There are no signs for us to see; there is no prophet left; there is not one among us who knows how long."[2]

I am amazed that someone could read the psalms and open them to present reality, thus opening present reality to prayer. It is important to note at the outset that Bonhoeffer taught that the psalms were to be prayed, prayed with Christ, whose prayers he believed they really were—in this case, with the Christ whose "weakest and most defenseless brothers" (as he called the Jews of Germany) were being persecuted.

A few days later, in a circular letter to pastors in the Confessing Church, Bonhoeffer wrote: "I have been thinking a great deal about Psalm 74, Zech. 2:8, and Rom. 9:4f. and 11:11-15. That leads us into very earnest prayer." He wanted them to look up those passages and to heed especially God's words about his people Israel in Zechariah 2:8—"Whoever touches you touches the apple of my eye."[3]

I would suggest, then, that the first lesson to be learned from these scriptural meditations by Dietrich Bonhoeffer is that the daily reading of Holy Scripture can affect the way in which we experience our social and political reality. Put another way, the Word incorporates our own experience into the history of salvation. Invited by Bonhoeffer's example, I have sensed this most vividly in my encounters with the church in Latin America. When I was privileged to travel with Salvadoran war refugees on their return home from the Mesa Grande refugee camp in Honduras, I caught some of the way they heard the words of Scripture. In their worship services, all that the Bible contains about returning from exile became living words for them.

Padre Serrano, an Episcopal priest from San Salvador, preached at a eucharist in the camp from the Lukan story about the return of the Holy Family from Egypt. The return of this holy family of the poor to their homes, he said, was differentiated only by the fact that their Herod was still on the throne.

The chief text that I took away from this journey of solidarity and fellowship with people from war-torn El Salvador was read in an open-air eucharist at the camp:

> In former generations this was not disclosed to the human race; but now it has been revealed by inspiration to his dedicated apostles and prophets, that through the Gospel the Gentiles are joint heirs with the Jews, part of the same body, sharers together in the promise made in Christ Jesus. Such is the gospel of which I was made a minister. (Ephesians 3:5-7)

In Spanish the words I heard were these: *"que los gentiles son coherederos y miembros del mismo cuerpo, y coparticipes de la promesa in Cristo Jesus."* In my mind and heart I substituted for *los gentiles* (the Gentiles), *los pobres* (the poor), and asked myself what it means for us if these refugees and all the other poor *campesinos* of Central America are *coherederos,* joint heirs, with us.

When we turn our attention to what Bonhoeffer teaches concerning our subjective response to God's Word, we dare not isolate that from the requirement to hear and obey the Word in the given social and political context. That would be like trying to separate what the epistle of James teaches about the "implanted word" from that epistle's prophetic outcry on behalf of the poor and the exploited workers. It would be separating gospel from law. But we know that Bonhoeffer's great gift as a theologian was his ability to find the gospel *in* the law, or to find freedom in obedience.

"Only he who cries out for the Jews may sing Gregorian chants," said Bonhoeffer.[4] Today he might say that only those who speak out for the poor may know the consolation of God's Word. For the rest, if we are to take seriously what the prophet Amos says, "they shall run to and fro, to seek the word of the LORD, but they shall not find it" (Amos 8:12).

The Word in the Heart

"The heart of God opens itself to us in God's Word," Bonhoeffer wrote to a friend. And it is in our human hearts that he believed it should find its home. He lived in such intimate relationship with Scripture, reading and "praying it" daily, that he could hear it as a "burning word" spoken to him personally by Jesus; he could read it as a "love letter from God."[5]

In his "Meditation on Psalm 119," with which this collection ends, Bonhoeffer writes at the eleventh verse:

> I do not treasure God's promise in my understanding but in my heart. It is not to be analysed by my intellect, but to be pondered in my heart.... Therefore, it is never sufficient simply to have read God's Word. It must penetrate deep

within us, dwell in us, like the Holy of Holies in the Sanctuary, so that we do not sin in thought, word, or deed.

His little book *Psalms: The Prayer Book of the Bible,* the last book he was allowed to publish under the Hitler regime, contains these instructions about how to read Psalm 119. They can serve, I think, as his guide to reading of any passage of Scripture.

Psalm 119 will be especially difficult for us, perhaps, because of its length and uniformity. Here a very slow, quiet, patient advance from word to word, from sentence to sentence, will help us. Then we will recognize that the apparent repetitions are ever new variations on a single theme—love for God's Word. As this love can never end, neither can the words which confess it. They are to accompany us through an entire lifetime and, in their simplicity, become the prayer of the child, the adult and the old person.[6]

Regular, meditative reading of the Bible was practiced by Bonhoeffer from the time when, as a young theologian, he became a Christian. "Becoming a Christian" seems, in fact, to have been the result of his discovering the Bible as the personal message of God's love for us. When we read his biography, as well as key passages such as those quoted above, it seems that the text from the epistle of James is most appropriate to describe Bonhoeffer's spirituality. He received with meekness the implanted Word, which was able to save his soul.

This reception of the Word was a daily, indeed almost a constant affair—since texts and single words of Scripture were kept and pondered in his heart. Such reading and meditating on the Word became for him a means of grace, differentiated from yet closely akin to hearing the Word preached in the congregation.

It was also a means of determining God's will for his life, as the "Meditation on Psalm 119" makes clear. There the words of Scripture are understood as Torah, God's guidance and direction for his followers. In James's terms, the Word is to be done, not simply heard.

Finally, such meditative reading of Scripture led him directly to prayer. The Bible was the school of prayer for Bonhoeffer, a school in which we learn the language of God, and "repeating God's own words after him, we begin to pray to God." The value placed upon each word, each passage, and a slow measured movement from word to word is stressed again by him in this context when he says: "The words which come from God will be the steps upon which we find our way to God."[7]

I will resist any further comment or paraphrase of his approach to meditative reading, and simply invite you to let Dietrich Bonhoeffer teach in his own words in the material that follows. I believe this can be of great value to anyone who wishes to learn to read, pray, and even preach the words of Scripture.

Some of the material presented here is fragmentary, and it is certainly unpolished when compared to his books. The "Meditation on Psalm 119" was only carried as far as verse 21. For Psalm 50 we have only a sermon outline. The sermons, letters, and instructions on meditation collected here were written for particular occasions rather than for posterity, but it is my hunch that they may be all the more helpful to us because of their fragmentary and everyday nature.

In chapters of *Life Together* we find Bonhoeffer's directions for meditation and prayer presented in a much more complete way. That lovely book should certainly be read. Yet a finished work like that may be almost too complete and well-rounded for us, with all of its instructions for life in community. The community of ordinands of the Confessing Church in Germany about which he is writing no longer exists. That period in the history of Europe, of the German church, and of Lutheran piety seems remote; the completed works of that time we may be tempted simply to read and place on our history shelf.

In examining these unfinished pieces, on the other hand, we may feel freer to pick up hints and insights that fit with the broken pieces of our own life and worship. The great point, after all, is not to take up Bonhoeffer and read him for his own sake, but to "take up and read" God's Word in our day as he did in his. The command spoken once to St. Augustine, *"tolle et lege,"* is a command to each generation of Christians. Observing how Dietrich Bonhoeffer obeyed it on a day-to-day basis, during his lifetime and in his work as a pastor, teacher, and political activist, can motivate us, I believe, to do the same.

Psalm 119

I find almost everything Bonhoeffer wrote based on the psalms helpful in coming to understand that special intimate relationship with God's Word that he attained and was able to pass on to others. The reminiscences of Hans-Werner Jensen, one of his seminary students at Gross Schlonwitz in 1938, point to the importance of the psalms and recapitulate some of what has been said thus far:

> Everyone knows today that Bonhoeffer saw daily meditation as one of the most central tasks for the theologian. The psalter was an absolutely essential part of such meditation. [I came to see at Gross-Schlonwitz] the meaning of the psalms as the prayers of the Church, the people of God, in the wilderness. I was happy to have learned this in seminary in order to be able to practice it later in the Gestapo prison. There are still some markings in my Bible from the time of Gross Schlonwitz, especially the date of 10 November 1938, *Kristallnacht:* "They burned down all the meeting-places of God in the land" (Ps. 74:7).[8]

But of all the psalms it was above all Psalm 119 that claimed Bonhoeffer's special attention. Bethge writes of a period in 1938 when Bonhoeffer was free to devote himself "with extraordinary concentration to his theological work. Now he was at last able to make some progress with his meditation on Psalm 119. He had learned at university that this was the most boring of psalms; now he regarded its interpretation as the climax of his theological life. He had been trying for years to penetrate into the mystery of its verses."[9]

The "Meditation on Psalm 119" is also of great biographical interest. Bethge writes:

> It was only later that friends discovered in expositions such as, for example, the meditation on Psalm 119, turns of speech that hinted at what was to come. Afterwards they recalled conversations such as the one on his thirty-third birthday on 4th February 1939...when he said that it might be worthwhile, even for a pastor, to risk one's life for political freedom.[10]

The reference is to his commentary on verse 1: "Happy are they whose way is blameless, who walk in the law of the LORD!"

> Yet it may be that God will give to one of his own the cup of suffering for Christ's sake.... Should God require this of any, he will certainly so prepare their hearts beforehand that they will be the very ones who by their strong faith testify anew and with authority: "Happy are they who walk in the law of the LORD!"

I have already quoted the special instructions for reading this psalm given in *Psalms: The Prayer Book of the Bible*. It may be well to sketch the general approach to the psalms taken in that book so that all the meditations can be read in that context. As the title of the book indicates, Bonhoeffer recognized the psalter as the prayer book of the church. But this recognition caused problems. How can sinful men and women pray the psalms of innocence (Pss. 5, 7, 9)? How can Christian people pray the psalms of vengeance (54, 55, 58)? How can those who have suffered little pray the psalms of those who suffered so much (13, 31, 35)? He solved these problems by understanding the psalms as the prayers of Christ. It is the innocent one who prays, the one who suffered for us. We pray, too, but only "in so far as Christ prays within us, not in our own name, but in the name of Jesus Christ."[11]

As we will see in his sermon on Psalm 58, this idea can become rather convoluted: the vengeance wished upon enemies in the psalm becomes the vengeance of God for human sin taken upon himself by Christ on the cross, thereby enabling him to pray for the forgiveness of enemies. But one need not accept such a complicated theological formula to be able to appreciate the breakthrough to a new level of intimacy with Scripture when Bonhoeffer writes: "We, too, can pray these psalms through Jesus Christ, from the heart of Jesus Christ."[12]

This perspective having been established, he next comments briefly on the various themes dealt with in the psalter. One of these themes is the law, which is celebrated especially in Psalms 1, 19, and 119. Bonhoeffer's love for God's law is always surprising, since the Lutheran *sola gratia* ("grace alone") might seem to stand in the way of such a wholehearted embrace. But he always found grace in the law. "It is grace to know God's commands. They release us from self-made plans and conflicts. They make our steps certain and our way joyful."[13] In a meditation on the ten commandments written in Tegel Prison in 1944, Bonhoeffer stressed the importance of the first words of the commandments: "I am the LORD your God, who brought you out of the land of Egypt, out of the house of bondage" (Ex. 20:2):

> God's first word in the ten commandments is "I." It is with this "I" that the human being has to do, not with any kind of general law; not with "one ought to do this and that," but with the living God. In each word of the ten commandments, God is really speaking about himself, and that is the most important thing about them. Hence, they are God's revelation. We do not obey a law in the ten commandments, we obey God. And when we transgress them we will not be brought to ruin by a law but by God himself.... Hence, the New Testament calls the ten commandments "living words."

> In truth, it is these first words which are the most important of all, the key to the ten commandments; they show us wherein God's commandments are to be eternally distinguished from human laws. In the ten commandments God expresses his grace as much as his command. They are not detachable, as if we could somehow separate God's will from God himself; rather, in them the complete, living God reveals himself as the one he is. That is the important thing.[14]

This understanding of the law is amplified in his
"Meditation on Psalm 119"; the understanding of
Holy Scripture as the living words of a living God is
found in all of Bonhoeffer's works.

His focus on this psalm in praise of God's law was
to some extent the result of his exposure to Anglican
spirituality. From 1933 to 1935, Bonhoeffer served as
pastor of a German congregation in London. Toward
the end of his stay in England and just before taking
up his duties as head of a seminary for the Confessing
Church, he decided to visit various seminaries and
religious communities in England. Among those he
visited was the Community of the Resurrection at
Mirfield. Bethge writes: "He went to Mirfield, where
he joined in the horary prayers during which Psalm
119 was recited on every day of the week; this was sub-
sequently to be the Bible passage most frequently
quoted by Bonhoeffer." And when, in 1938, he settled
down to concentrated work on Psalm 119, he wrote to
a close friend asking his help in obtaining a copy of
The Way of Holiness by Richard Meux Benson, the
nineteenth-century founder of the Society of St. John
the Evangelist at Cowley, Oxford. "I need it for the
exposition of Psalm 119," he wrote.[15]

I do not know how many of Father Benson's works
were known to Bonhoeffer, but they contain insights
that would certainly have impressed him and con-
firmed him in his own approach to Scripture. Benson
advocated a lively and personal appropriation of the
psalms by means of prayer and meditation, just as
Bonhoeffer did. In his devotional commentary on the
psalter, *The War Songs of the Prince of Peace,* published
in 1901, Benson writes: "We must see that we use the

Psalter as no mere venerable tradition of ages which have passed away, but in the living fellowship of heavenly joy, whereby the children of grace ought to feel their union with the incarnate Word." He speaks elsewhere of the necessity of accustoming ourselves to a "practical familiarity with the Psalter, bringing it in so as to meet the wants of daily life, finding in the wants of daily life a real opportunity of sympathy with our Lord Jesus Christ."[16]

Furthermore, Benson's introduction to his own exposition of Psalm 119 includes these words concerning Christ's ownership of the psalms. They could have come directly from Bonhoeffer:

> Sometimes it seems as if the words were ours, and Jesus put them into our lips that we might speak them as taught by Him. Sometimes the words seem to be primarily or wholly His own, so that we can only speak them as His members.[17]

As the letters and instructions in this collection will reveal, Bonhoeffer was continually being asked to set down his method for meditating on Scripture. It is refreshing to see how simple the method was: "Accept the Word of Scripture and ponder it in your heart as Mary did. That is all. That is meditation."

On the Translation
Since my goal is to make these writings available to men and women in the church as an aid to their own reading of Scripture, it did not seem to make sense to

translate the German Bible text into English. Instead, it seemed more helpful to use *The Book of Common Prayer* text for the psalms and the *Revised Standard Version* for other Scripture passages, except in those few instances where the German Bible text used by Bonhoeffer yields a quite different meaning. I have indicated in editorial notes where I have stayed with the German. Of course, to do it this way means that in some passages of Bonhoeffer's commentary I have had to translate more freely so that the end result would be the kind of word-by-word exposition that Bonhoeffer's method calls for. I think that any such departure from the letter is done in accord with his own "Instructions in Daily Meditation," where he tells his seminarians to use the text most familiar to them, in their case the Luther text.

I have exercised one other liberty in translating by alternating the use of masculine and feminine pronouns in some of the meditations. I indicate in the editorial notes when the pronouns vary from the original in this way. I have chosen to do this for those meditations that I have judged to be of the greatest value to our contemporary devotions, that is, the meditations on Psalm 42, Psalm 34:19, and Psalm 119. The remaining material I have left alone. Among these pieces there are, however, interesting exceptions to the masculine rhetoric: the funeral sermon for his grandmother, and the passage in "Morning" in which God is referred to as our mother.

Translators of poetry and meditative writings are granted a fair amount of freedom, so that they can produce something that is lovely to read in their own language. I have claimed a little more freedom than that, in the name of Christ.

None of the above excuses any errors I might have made in capturing the letter or the spirit of Dietrich Bonhoeffer. For any such errors, as all translators should, I ask your forgiveness.

DAVID McI. GRACIE,
Philadelphia, Pennsylvania

*These translations are offered in thanksgiving for
the deepening relationship between
the Episcopal Church and the
Evangelical Lutheran Church in America.*

I

ON MEDITATION

Early in the morning I cry out to you,
  for in your word is my trust.
My eyes are open in the night watches,
  that I may meditate upon your promise.

Psalm 119:147-148

*

INSTRUCTIONS IN DAILY MEDITATION

The Confessing Church was formed in 1934 at the Barmen Synod. There, representatives from German regional churches severed themselves from the national church, which was serving Hitler's purposes, and they set forth their own understanding of the gospel in the famous Barmen Declaration.

This Confessing Church called Dietrich Bonhoeffer home from London in 1935 to take responsibility for training some of its ordinands at a seminary that was established at Finkenwalde, near the Baltic Sea. The "Instructions in Daily Meditation" have their origin there. They were written down by Eberhard Bethge, the seminarian who was later to become Bonhoeffer's biographer and the editor of his collected works. Bethge attached them to a circular letter sent to Confessing Church pastors from Finkenwalde on May 22, 1936. The letter shared news about colleagues who had been imprisoned by the Nazis.

In the biography, Bethge tells us how the requirement by Bonhoeffer that seminarians devote a half-hour each morning to silent meditation on a Scripture text caused them great difficulties. They did not know how to use the time. Some went to sleep, some daydreamed, others worked on sermons. These instructions were intended to make clear to the seminarians the importance of individual meditation and the manner in which it was to be done.

Communal meditation was also practiced once a week at the seminary. Even in individual meditation Bonhoeffer tried to build a sense of community by encouraging the use of a common text. After the seminarians had left Finkenwalde they continued to receive suggested texts for common meditation in the circular letters.

In a letter to Karl Barth in 1936, Bonhoeffer wrote: "The kind of questions serious young theologians put to us are: How can I learn to pray? How can I learn to read the Bible? Either we can help them to do this, or we can't help them at all. Nothing of all this can be taken for granted."[18]

1. Why do I meditate?

Because I am a Christian. Therefore, every day in which I do not penetrate more deeply into the knowledge of God's Word in Holy Scripture is a lost day for me. I can only move forward with certainty upon the firm ground of the Word of God. And, as a Christian, I learn to know the Holy Scripture in no other way than by hearing the Word preached and by prayerful meditation.

Because I am a preacher of the Word. I cannot expound the Scripture for others if I do not let it speak daily to me. I will misuse the Word in my office as preacher if I do not continue to meditate upon it in prayer. If the Word has become empty for me in my daily administrations, if I no longer experience it, that proves I have not let the Word speak personally to me for a long time. I will offend against my calling if I do not seek each day in prayer the word that my Lord wants to say to me for that day. Ministers of the Word are especially called upon to perform the office of prayer: "But we will devote ourselves to prayer and to the ministry of the word" (Acts 6:4). The pastor must pray more than others, and has more to pray about.

Because I need a firm discipline of prayer. We like to pray according to our moods—briefly, at length, or not at all. But that is to be arbitrary. Prayer is not a free-will offering to God; it is an obligatory service, something that he requires. We are not free to engage in it according to our own wishes. Prayer is the first divine service in the day. God requires that we take time for this service. "Early in the morning I cry out to you, for in your word is my trust. My eyes are open in the night watches, that I may meditate upon your promise" (Ps. 119:147-148). "Seven times a day do I praise you, because of your righteous judgments" (Ps. 119:164). God needed time before he came to us in Christ for our salvation. He needs time before he comes into my heart for my salvation.

Because I need help against the ungodly haste and unrest that threaten my work as a pastor. Only from the peace of God's Word can there flow the proper, devoted service of each day.

2. What do I want from my meditation?

We want in any case to rise up from our meditation in a different state from when we sat down. We want to meet Christ in his Word. We turn to the text in our desire to hear what it is that he wants to give us and teach us today through his Word. Meet him first in the day, before you meet other people. Every morning lay upon him everything that preoccupies you and weighs you down, before new burdens are laid upon you. Ask yourself what still hinders you from following him completely and let him take charge of that, before new hindrances are placed in your way.

His fellowship, his help, his guidance for the day through his Word—that is the goal. Thus you will begin the day freshly strengthened in your faith.

3. How shall I meditate?

There is free meditation and meditation that is bound to Scripture. We advise the latter for the sake of the certainty of our prayers and the discipline of our thoughts. Furthermore, the knowledge of our fellowship with others who are meditating on the same text will make us love such meditation more.

In the same way that the word of a person who is dear to me follows me throughout the day, so the Word of Scripture should resonate and work within me ceaselessly. Just as you would not dissect and analyze the word spoken by someone dear to you, but would accept it just as it was said, so you should accept the Word of Scripture and ponder it in your heart as Mary did. That is all. That is meditation. Do not look for new thoughts and interconnections in the text as you would in a sermon! Do not ask how you should tell it to others, but ask what it tells you! Then ponder this word in your heart at length, until it is entirely within you and has taken possession of you.

It is not necessary every day to go through the entire text we have chosen for meditation. Often we will hold on to one word of it for the entire day. Passages that we do not understand we can simply pass over. There is no need to take flight into philology. This is not the place for the Greek New Testament, but for the familiar Luther text.

If during meditation our thoughts move to persons who are near to us or to those we are concerned about, then let them linger there. That is a good time to pray for them. Do not pray in general, then, but in particular for the people who are on your mind. Let the Word of Scripture tell you what you ought to pray for them. As a help, we may write down the names of the people we want to remember every day. Our intercessions require their appointed time, too, if we are to be serious about them. Pay attention, though, that our intercessions do not become another means of taking flight from the most important thing: prayer for our own soul's salvation.

We begin our meditations with the prayer for the Holy Spirit, asking for proper concentration for ourselves and for all who we know are also meditating. Then we turn to the text. At the close of the meditation we want to be truly able to say a prayer of thanksgiving from a heart that is full.

What text, and how long should the text be? It has proven helpful to meditate on a text of approximately ten to fifteen verses for a period of a week. It is not good to meditate on a different text each day, since we are not always equally receptive, and the texts for the most part are much too long for that. Whatever you do, do not take the sermon text for the next Sunday. That belongs in your sermon meditation time. It is a great help if a community knows that it is concentrating all week on the same text.

The time of meditation is in the morning before the beginning of our work. A half-hour is the minimum amount of time that a proper meditation requires. It is, of course, necessary that there be complete quiet, and that we intend to allow nothing to divert us, no matter how important it may seem.

Occasional meditation with two or more people is quite possible in a Christian community, although, sadly, it is seldom practiced. In such meditation there is a narrow way that leads between false, pious talk and idle theological discussion.

4. How do we overcome the problems of meditation?

Whoever seriously undertakes the daily practice of meditation will soon discover great difficulties. Meditation and prayer must be practiced earnestly and for a long time. So the first rule is not to become impatient with yourself. Do not become confused and upset because of your distractedness. Just sit down again every day and wait very patiently. If your thoughts keep wandering, there is no need for you to hold on to them compulsively. There is nothing wrong with letting them roam where they will; but then incorporate in your prayers the place or person to which they have gone. So you will find your way back to your text, and the minutes spent in such diversions will not be lost and will no longer be any cause for worry.

There are many helps for special difficulties that each one may use. Read the same passage again and again, write down your thoughts, learn the verse by heart (indeed, you will memorize any text that has been thoroughly meditated upon). But in all this we soon learn to recognize the danger of fleeing once again from meditation to Bible scholarship or the like. Behind all our uncertainties and needs stands our great need to pray; for all too long many of us have known this need without finding any help or direction. The only help is to faithfully and patiently begin again our earliest exercises of prayer and meditation. We will be further helped by the knowledge that other brothers are also meditating, that at all times the entire holy church in heaven and on earth prays with us. That is a comfort to us in the weakness of our own prayers. And if we really do not know what we ought to pray and completely lose heart about it, we still know that the Holy Spirit prays for us with "groanings which cannot be uttered" (Rom. 8:26).

We dare not allow ourselves to cease from this daily engagement with the Scripture, and we must begin it right away if it is not now our practice. For in doing so we have eternal life.

MORNING

The community life of the seminarians at Finkenwalde lasted less than two and a half years because the Gestapo closed the seminary doors in September 1937. But this brief experiment in the religious life of Protestant Germany attracted much attention. Bonhoeffer's little book Life Together, *published in 1939, was the most widely read of his books during his lifetime. Bethge described it as a work that contained "the outlines of a living Protestant community."* Life Together *presented in more finished form what had only been sketched out in the "Instructions in Daily Meditation" and in the following draft, dated 1935 or 1936 in the collected works, and entitled simply "Morning."[19]*

Each morning is a new beginning of our life. Each day is a finished whole. The present day marks the boundary of our cares and concerns (Mt. 6:34, Jas. 4:14). It is long enough to find God or to lose him, to keep faith or fall into disgrace. God created day and night for us so we need not wander without boundaries, but may be able to see every morning the goal of the evening ahead. Just as the ancient sun rises anew every day, so the eternal mercy of God is new every morning (Lam. 3:23). Every morning God gives us the gift of comprehending anew his faithfulness of old; thus, in the midst of our life with God, we may daily begin a new life with him.

In Holy Scripture, morning is a time full of wonder. It is the time of God's help for his church (Ps. 46:5), the time of joy after a night of weeping (Ps. 30:5), the time of the proclamation of the divine Word (Zeph. 3:5), the daily distribution of the sacred manna (Ex. 16:13f.). Before daybreak Jesus went away to pray (Mk. 1:35), in the early hours the women go to the tomb, and the disciples find the risen Jesus on the shore of the Lake of Tiberias (Jn. 21:4). The people of faith wake early because of their expectation of God's marvelous acts (Gen. 19:27, Ex. 24:4, Job 1:5, etc.). Sleep no longer holds them. They rush to greet the early grace of God.

When we awake, we drive away the dark shapes and confused dreams of the night as we speak the morning blessing and commend ourselves for this day to the triune God. The evil moods, uncontrollable emotions, and desires that we cannot get rid of during the day are often enough simply ghosts of the night that were not driven off in the morning and now want to spoil the day for us. The first moments of the new day are not the time for our own plans and worries, not even for our zeal to accomplish our own work, but for God's liberating grace, God's sanctifying presence. To anyone who is wakened early by care, Scripture says: "It is in vain that you rise so early and go to bed so late; vain, too, to eat the bread of toil" (Ps. 127:3). It is not my anxiety about the coming day, not the burden of my work that I have before me, but it is the Lord who wakes me every morning; "he wakens my ear to hear as those who are taught" (Is. 50:4). Before the heart unlocks itself for the world, God wants to open it for himself; before the ear takes in the countless voices of the day, it should hear in the early hours the voice of the Creator and Redeemer. God prepared the stillness of the first morning for himself. It should remain his.

Before our daily bread should be the daily Word. Only thus will the bread be received with thanksgiving. Before our daily work should be the morning prayer. Only thus will the work be done as the fulfillment of God's command. The morning must yield an hour of quiet time for prayer and common devotion. That is certainly not wasted time. How else could we prepare ourselves to face the tasks, cares, and temptations of the day? And although we are often not "in the mood" for it, such devotion is an obligatory service to the One who desires our praises and prayers, and who will not otherwise bless our day but through his Word and our prayers.

It is wrong to say that we are being "legalistic" when we are concerned with the ordering of our Christian life and with our faithfulness in requirements of Scripture reading and prayer. Disorder undermines and destroys the faith: any theologian who confuses evangelical freedom with lack of discipline needs to learn that. Whoever wants to carry out properly any fully developed spiritual office, without bringing both self and work to ruin by mere activism, must learn early on the spiritual discipline of the servant of Jesus Christ. The young theologian will find it a great help to set certain times for quiet prayers and for devotions, and to hold to them with patience and persistence.

Every Christian needs quiet time for prayer. The theologian who wants to be a Christian needs it more than anyone else. More time for God's Word and for prayer is needed because of our appointment to a special task (Acts 6:4). How should we go about during the day as ministers of the Word, preaching and instructing, helping to carry the burdens of others, if we have not experienced God's help for the day ourselves? We do not want our work to become routine and hollow. It is advisable to base the quiet time of prayer on a passage of Scripture. That provides content for our prayers and gives us confidence and ground to stand on. It can be the same portion of Scripture for a week. Then the Word can dwell in us and begin to come alive; consciously or unconsciously, it will be present with us wherever we go. A too quick change makes for superficiality. Grounded in the Scripture, we learn to speak to God in the language that God has spoken to us. We learn to speak to God as the child speaks to its mother.

Proceeding from the Word of God, we pray everything that the Word teaches us; we bring the coming day before God and cleanse our thoughts and intentions before him; we pray above all to be in full communion with Jesus Christ. We do not want to forget to pray for ourselves; "ascribe to yourself honor according to your worth" (Sir. 10:28). Next, the broad field of intercession lies before us. Here our view expands to see persons and things near and far, in order to commend them to the grace of God. No one who has requested our prayers may be left out. We must include all those who have been committed to our care either personally or professionally—and there are many. Finally, each of us knows of persons who otherwise would scarcely have anyone to pray for them. Nor should we forget to thank God for those who help and strengthen us by their intercessions. We do not want to conclude the quiet time of prayer before we have repeated the Amen with great conviction.

For our common devotions we seek housemates or others from the neighborhood in order to hear God's Word, to sing and to pray with them. Above all, we should read the psalms together. They can only become our possession if we read and pray them daily without omitting any, even when they are difficult. Then a not-too-modest portion of the Old and New Testaments should be read in series. The songs of the Church will place us in the great congregation of the present and the past. The prayer that one person speaks for the whole fellowship will bring the common concerns of the little house congregation before God.

Now God has spoken his Word in the silence of the morning; now we have found fellowship with God and with the congregation of Christians. We can go to our day's work with confidence.

✳

THE BIBLE ALONE

A Letter to Dr. Rudiger Schleicher

Rudiger Schleicher was Bonhoeffer's brother-in-law and good friend. They shared many interests, including music. Dietrich played the piano and would accompany Rudiger on the violin in sonatas of Beethoven and Mozart. While trained in the law, Schleicher was interested in theology. At the time of this letter, at least, his position was in line with the liberal school of Protestant teaching exemplified by Adolf Harnack. Dietrich had been a pupil of Harnack's but was now identifying more with Karl Barth in his rediscovery of the "strange new world of the Bible."

The early paragraphs of the letter allude to various criticisms by Schleicher of his brother-in-law's teaching and preaching. Bonhoeffer accepts the sincere intentions of his friendly critic and then proceeds to explain to him in increasingly personal terms his own approach to reading and appropriating the Word of God in the Bible.

In the first paragraph reference is made to Schleicher's having been laid up due to a wound he had suffered in World War I. He would not live to see the end of World War II. In the final month of the war he, like his brother-in-law, would be arrested and executed for participating in the conspiracy to kill Adolf Hitler.[20]

Friedrichsbrunn, 8 April 1936

Dear Rudiger!

Your letter just arrived. It pleased me so much to receive it that I want to respond right away. I am using the typewriter as an act of charity to you!—I didn't know that you were laid up again. Nowadays, with so much careless talk about war, that affects me in a special way.

Now to the main concern. We have often feuded with each other before, and until now it has always come out right. So it will again. I find it helpful to keep reminding myself that the pastor can never satisfy the proper "layman." If I preach faith and grace alone (as I did at Trinity Church!), then you ask: What about the Christian life? If I discuss the Sermon on the Mount (as I did in my lectures!), then you ask: What about real life? If I interpret the very real and sinful life of some person in the Bible, then you ask: Where are the eternal verities? And all these questions really express only one concern: How can I live a Christian life in the real world, and where are the final authorities for such a life, which alone is worth living?

First, I want to confess quite simply that I believe the Bible alone is the answer to all our questions, and that we only need to ask persistently and with some humility in order to receive the answer from it. One cannot simply read the Bible the way one reads other books. One must be prepared to really question it. Only then will it open itself up. Only when we await the final answer from the Bible will it be given to us. That is because in the Bible it is God who speaks to us. And we cannot simply reach our own conclusions about God; rather, we must ask him. He will only answer us if we are seeking after him. Naturally, one can also read the Bible like any other book—from the perspective of textual criticism, for instance. There is nothing to be said against that. But that will only reveal the surface of the Bible, not what is within it. When a dear friend speaks a word to us, do we subject it to analysis? No, we simply accept it, and then it resonates inside us for days. The word of someone we love opens itself up to us the more we "ponder it in our hearts," as Mary did. In the same way, we should carry the Word of the Bible around with us. We will only be happy in our reading of the Bible when we dare to approach it as the means by which God really speaks to us, the God who loves us and will not leave us with our questions unanswered.

Now, we can only seek for what we already know. If I do not know what I am really looking for, then I am not really looking for anything. So, we must already know which God we seek before we can look for him. If I do not know that, I will just rummage around, and seeking will become my main purpose instead of finding anything at all. So I can only find if I know what I seek. Now, I either know about the God I seek from my own experience and insights, from the meanings which I assign to history or nature—that is, from within myself—or I know about him based on his revelation of his own Word. Either I determine the place in which I will find God, or I allow God to determine the place where he will be found.

If it is I who say where God will be, I will always find there a God who in some way corresponds to me, is agreeable to me, fits in with my nature. But if it is God who says where he will be, then that will truly be a place that at first is not agreeable to me at all, that does not fit so well with me. That place is the cross of Christ. And whoever will find God there must draw near to the cross in the manner that the Sermon on the Mount requires. That does not correspond to our nature at all; it is, in fact, completely contrary to it. But this is the message of the Bible, not only the New Testament but also the Old (Is. 53!). In any case, Jesus and Paul understand it in this way—that the cross of Jesus fulfills the Scriptures of the Old Testament. The entire Bible, then, is the Word in which God allows himself to be found by us. Not a place that is agreeable to us or makes sense to us *a priori,* but instead a place that is strange to us and contrary to our nature. Yet, the very place in which God has decided to meet us.

This is how I read the Bible now. I ask of each passage: What is God saying to us here? And I ask God that he would help us hear what he wants to say. So, we no longer look for general, eternal truths, which correspond with our own "eternal" nature and are, therefore, somehow self-evident to us. Instead, we seek the will of God, who is altogether strange to us, whose

ways are not our ways and whose thoughts are not our
thoughts, who hides himself from us under the sign of
the cross, in which all our ways and thoughts have an
end. God is completely other than the so-called eternal verities. Theirs is an eternity made up of our own
thoughts and wishes. But God's Word begins by show-
ing us the cross. And it is to the cross, to death and
judgment before God, that our ways and thoughts
(even the "eternal" ones) all lead.

Does this perspective somehow make it understandable to you that I do not want to give up the Bible
as this strange Word of God at any point, that I intend
with all my powers to ask what God wants to say to us
here? Any other place outside the Bible has become
too uncertain for me. I fear that I will only encounter
some divine double of myself there. Does this somehow help you understand why I am prepared for a *sac-
rificium intellectus*—just in these matters, and only in
these matters, with respect to the one, true God! And
who does not bring to some passages his sacrifice of
the intellect, in the confession that he does not yet
understand this or that passage in Scripture, but is certain that even they will be revealed one day as God's
own Word? I would rather make that confession than
try to say according to my own opinion: this is divine,
that is human.

And now let me tell you quite personally that since
I learned to read the Bible in this way—and that is not
so long ago—it has become daily more wonderful to
me. I read it mornings and evenings, often also during
the day. And each day I take up a text, which I have
before me for the entire week, and I attempt to
immerse myself in it completely, in order to really lis-

ten to it. I know that without this I could no longer rightly live, let alone believe. And every day more riddles are solved for me, even though I am still just moving on the surface.

As I was looking at medieval art again in Hildesheim, it occurred to me how much more they understood about the Bible in those times. I am also struck by the fact that our ancestors in their battles for the faith had nothing, and wanted nothing, but the Bible, and that by means of the Bible they became strong and free for a real life of faith. It would be simply superficial, I think, to say that everything has changed since then. Human beings and their needs have remained the same. And the Bible answers those needs today no less than then. It may be that this sounds very primitive. But you have no idea how happy one can be to find one's way back from the false tracks of so much theology to these primitive things. And I believe that in matters of faith we are always equally primitive.

In a few days it will be Easter. That makes me very happy. But do you think that either of us by ourselves could believe or would want to believe these impossible things that are reported in the gospels, if the Bible did not support us in our belief? Simply the Word, as God's truth, which he vouches for himself. Resurrection—that is not a self-evident idea, an eternal verity. I mean, of course, resurrection as the Bible means it—as a rising up from real death (not sleep) to real life, from life without God to new life with Christ in God. God has said (and we know this through the Bible): "Behold I make all things new." He made that come true at Easter. Must not this message appear much more impossible, distant, unreal than the whole story of King David, which, by comparison, is quite harmless?

There remains, then, only the decision whether we will trust the Bible or not, whether we will allow ourselves to be supported by it as by no other word, in life and death. And I believe that we can only be happy and at peace when we have made that decision.

Forgive me, this has become a very long epistle. I do not know if I should write in this way. Yet I believe I should, and I am very pleased that we have had one such exchange of letters. We must go on sharing what we believe we have discovered. Whether we have a right to speak as I have now spoken to you will be proved in our experience. For now we must lay it aside.

With all good wishes and greetings to you all,

your Dietrich

FALLEN IN ACTION

A Letter in Wartime

1942 was a year of travel for Bonhoeffer. He went to Scandinavia and to Switzerland seeking some international understanding and support for the secret effort to topple the Hitler regime. Bethge writes that in that year it was "a race between assassination and arrest. His urgent private affairs ranged from making a will to deciding to become engaged."

In spite of the urgency of all this, he found time to correspond with the men he had once trained. As this letter indicates, a number of them were on the front lines and some had been killed. He writes to the brothers once again about the central importance of prayer and meditation on Scripture, which, even in the midst of war, could be their source of peace.[21]

March 1, 1942

Dear Brother....

Our dear brothers Bruno Kerlin, Gerhard Vibrans, and Gerhard Lehne have been killed in action. They sleep now with all the brothers who have gone before them, awaiting the great Easter Day of the Resurrection. We see the cross and we believe in the Resurrection; see death and we believe in eternal life; we experience sadness and separation but we believe in eternal joy and fellowship. Bruno Kerlin was a witness to this Easter faith by his own joyful faith, the clarity of his nature and his willingness to serve the community. For that we thank God. Gerhard Vibrans was hit by a bomb from a plane just as he was about to sing some hymns with his comrades. Anyone who knew this sincere, selfless brother, who so combined simplicity and maturity that he was trusted by so many different people, will know what we have lost in him. The text for the day of his death, February 3, moved me deeply. "The hair of his head was white as snow-white wool, and his eyes flamed like fire" (Rev. 1:14). The life of this brother was lived under the flaming eyes of Christ; it was a reflection of this purifying flame. I will never forget that he taught me the hymn of Claudius: "I thank God and rejoice...." His life was a powerful exposition of that hymn. Gerhard Lehne was a searching, wandering, restless person of many interests and experiences, and with all that, a man of great candor and simple honesty. The goal that held him fast illuminated everything he did. He did

his work in the church selflessly and faithfully. Now
God has taken him to an early rest and to peace. We
praise and thank God for the lives and deaths of our
brothers. Their deaths make us realize the blessing
that God has given us through our fellowship in his
Word and at his Table. They also admonish us to
prove faithful to one another as long as we are able to
do so.

I have experienced this faithfulness in these last
weeks in an overpowering way. I can never express my
thankfulness for this in words alone. For the whole
month I have been receiving letters for my birthday
from those who are performing difficult service at
home and also from those in the bitter cold of Russia;
sometimes they are written during brief pauses in the
fighting. How shall I respond to such faithfulness? I
thank you from the bottom of my heart. Let us remain
constant in prayer for one another. Who knows how
much protection through God's grace he owes to the
intercession of a brother?

I have been surprised to see that the number of
those asking for additional help with regard to meditation has increased just recently. I confess that I
would not have dared to speak to you about that on
my own. I would not want to add one more burden to
those you are bearing every day. So even now I will do
no more than say a few words again about the precious
gift that is given to us in meditation and how it is especially important for us today. Daily, quiet reflection on
the Word of God as it applies to me (even if only for a
few minutes) becomes for me a point of crystallization
for everything that gives interior and exterior order to
my life. Our previous ordered life has been broken up

and dissolved in these present days, and we are in danger of losing our inner sense of order, too, because of the rush of events, the demands of work, doubts, temptations, conflicts, and unrest of all kinds. Meditation can give to our lives a measure of steadiness; it can preserve the link to our previous existence, from baptism to confirmation to ordination; it can keep us in the wholesome fellowship of the congregation, of our brothers, of our spiritual home; it can be a spark from that hearth fire that the congregations want to keep tending for you at home. Meditation is a source of peace, of patience, and of joy; it is like a magnet that draws together all the forces in our life that make for order; it is like deep water that reflects the clouds and the sun on its clear surface. It also serves the Most High by presenting him with a place of discipline, stillness, healing, and contentment in our lives. Have we not all a deep, perhaps unconfessed, longing for such a gift? Could it not become for us once more a source of health and strength? For a variety of reasons I think it best at present if we keep to the old epistles for our meditation. May God bless these hours for us.

Today on the first of March we had a warm spring sun for the first time; the snow is dripping from the roofs, the air is clear, and one can see the earth again. Our thoughts are with you who have undergone such unimaginable things in the past months of winter on the front. Our wish for you is that you too will soon be cheered by the return of the sun with its warmth, and by the sight of the earth.

He gives snow like wool;
   he scatters hoarfrost like ashes.
He scatters his hail like bread crumbs;
   who can stand against his cold?
He sends forth his word and melts them;
   he blows with his wind, and the waters flow.

                               (Ps. 147:17-19)

One day he will also bring to an end the winter and dark night of evil and allow a springtime of grace and joy to return. "Summer is near at hand, the winter is past, the tender blossoms appear; he who has begun this work will also bring it to completion" (Luther).

In the confidence and fellowship of this faith, I commend you to God and to our Lord Jesus Christ.

                               Faithfully yours,
                            Dietrich Bonhoeffer

II

SERMONS ON
THE PSALMS

＊

ON PSALM 62

Sermon for the 6th Sunday after Trinity,
July 15, 1928

Dietrich Bonhoeffer was twenty-two years of age when he preached this sermon. He was serving as assistant pastor to a German congregation in Barcelona. According to Bethge, he took his pastoral duties very seriously, especially his preaching. The youthful sermons tended to be flowery in their language and lofty in their themes, sometimes passing over the heads of his congregation.

This sermon on a psalm text may be of value in the present collection because it shows Bonhoeffer's early interest in meditation. When compared with his instructions in meditation to his seminarians in 1936, we can clearly see his growth. It is striking to see the way he minimizes the role of Scripture in meditation in this sermon. In his later work meditation was always bound to Scripture: "Schriftgebundene Meditation" is what he taught and practiced. The conversion to the Bible, which he would write about in the letter to Rudiger Schleicher, had obviously not yet taken place in 1928.

But for all of that, we find here a strong endorsement of the psalmist's call for silence before God, which is the precondition for meditation of any kind. [22]

Psalm 62

1 For God alone my soul in silence waits;
   from him comes my salvation.

Thousands of years ago, a devout person, tossed about by the storms of life, knelt down before God in the silence of the Jewish Temple. Only when this sacred silence had penetrated the depths of his soul was he able to say these words: "For God alone my soul in silence waits; from him comes my salvation." Oh, you ancient singer, you appear to us like an image from a pleasant dream that we long for, yet find so distant from us. We are attracted to you, but we no longer understand you. Teach us something about the silence of the soul, the soul that waits for God.

As the infant becomes still upon its mother's breast, as the youth is silent when he looks up to his heroes, as the crying child longs for the mother's hand to be laid upon its brow to banish all its cares, as the husband finds his anxiety stilled in the glance of his beloved wife, as true friends become silent when looking into each other's eyes, as a sick person is set at ease by the doctor's presence, as older people become still in the face of death, so our souls are to be stilled from their unrest, agitation, and hurriednesss before the eyes of God. Our thirst is to be quenched, our desires become true happiness, as we find our rest from the heat of the day in the shadow of God's hand. Our souls are to cast off care and burdens and find freedom in the glance of God; they are to be silent in reverence and adoration. "For God alone my soul in silence waits."

Being silent means being unable to say anything more; it means that a strange but dear hand has placed itself upon our lips to make us be still; it means giving ourselves totally—capitulating to the overwhelming power of the Other, the totally Other; it means for a moment no longer seeing oneself at all, but only the Other. But it also means waiting, waiting for the Other to say something to us. Being silent before God means making room for God so that he may speak the first and last word about us, and then receiving that word, whatever it may be, for all eternity; it means not wanting to justify ourselves, but wanting to hear whether God wishes to say something about our justification. To be silent does not mean to be inactive, rather it means to breathe in the will of God, to listen attentively and be ready to obey. The time of silence is a time of responsibility, a time when we must answer to God and to ourselves; but it is also a time of blessedness, because it is a time when we live in the peace of God. "For God alone my soul in silence waits." That means: "Speak, Lord, for your servant hears."

"For God alone my soul in silence waits; *from him comes my salvation.*" God's times are times of salvation. God has an answer ready, and this answer is one and the same to whomever it is given: to the woman who has put behind her the hustle and bustle of everyday life, to the sick man who comes before God in his misery, to the one who is mourning the loss of a loved one, and to all who are guilt-laden. To man and woman, old person and child, God speaks his winning word: I love you. To be sure, the fire of God's love burns up all that is evil and false in the human heart, and that causes pain. To be silent before God means to be humbled before God, to feel the pain of contrition; but, beyond all measure, there is the joy of love and grace. "For God alone my soul in silence waits; from him comes my salvation." If our soul has found the way to him, then he saves us, as sure as he is God.

Oh, well, some will say, you are telling us about beautiful things once more, but why is it that only so few come to realize them?

There are two simple reasons for that. First, we are so afraid of silence that we chase ourselves from one event to the next in order not to have to spend a moment alone with ourselves, in order not to have to look at ourselves in the mirror. We know that those times when we have to be alone are often the most comfortless and fruitless of times for us. But we are not only afraid of ourselves and of self-discovery, we are much more afraid of God—that he may disturb us and discover who we really are, that he may take us with him into his solitude and deal with us according to his will. We are afraid of such lonely, awful encounters with God, and we avoid them, so that he may not suddenly come too near to us. It would be too dreadful to have to face God directly, to have to answer to him. Our smiles would have to disappear; for once, something would have to be taken seriously, and we are not used to that. This anxiety is a mark of our times; we live in fear that we may suddenly find ourselves before the Eternal.

That is one reason. The other is that we are too indolent in our religious life. Perhaps we once made a start, but how soon we went to sleep again. We say we are not in the mood, and since religion is a matter of mood, we must wait until it overtakes us. And then we wait and wait for years, perhaps to the end of our lives, until we once again are in the mood for religion. There is a great deception behind all of this. We may regard religion as a matter of mood if we wish, but God is not determined by our moods; one does not wait until overtaken by a feeling to encounter him. The person who waits upon moods is impoverished. If the painter only wanted to paint when in the mood for it, he would not get very far. In religion, as in art and science, along with the times of high excitement, there are times of sober work and practice. We must practice our communication with God, otherwise we will not find the right tone, the right word, the right language, when God surprises us with his presence. We must learn the language of God, carefully learn it, work hard at it, so that we will be able to speak to him. Prayer must be practiced. It is a fatal error to confuse religion with sentimentality. Religion is work, perhaps the most difficult and certainly the holiest work that a human being can do. How miserable to be content with saying, "I am not religiously inclined," when there is a God who wants to have us as his own. It is simply an evasion. Certainly, it will be harder for one person than for another, but we may be sure that no one can advance without work. This is why even our silence before God takes practice and work; it takes daily fortitude to expose ourselves to God's Word and to allow ourselves to be judged by it; it requires daily renewal as we rejoice in the love of God.

With that we are led to ask: What do we need to do in order to reach this state of silent waiting for God? In answer, I can only say a little out of my quite modest experience. None of us is so rushed that it would be impossible to allow for even ten minutes in the day, in the morning or the evening, in which arrangements could be made for silence, in order to place oneself in the presence of Eternity, allow it to speak, question it, and thereby look deep within and far beyond oneself. One might have a few verses of the Bible to read, but it is best to freely allow the soul to take its own way to the Father's house, to the homeland in which it finds peace. Whoever earnestly works at this day by day will be overwhelmed by the golden harvest of the fruit of those times.

Certainly, any beginning is difficult, and whoever begins such an undertaking will experience the first attempts as strange and perhaps completely empty. But that cannot continue for long; the soul will fill itself, it will begin to revive and gain strength. Then it will experience the eternal silence that rests in the love of God. Cares and sorrows, unrest and haste, noise and confusion, dreams and anxieties—all will be stilled in that silence, in which the soul waits for God alone, from whom comes its salvation.

It is a law of the world that there can never be rest and satisfaction here. Here no passion will ever be completely stilled. Every satisfaction has planted within itself that which drives beyond what has been achieved. The rich person wants to become richer, the mighty one mightier. The reason for this is that in the world there is never anything completely whole, so that each success, no matter how great, is only a partial success. If it is possible for there to be rest and silence anywhere, then it is only possible where there is wholeness, and that is only in God. All human strivings and drives are finally directed toward God and can only find their complete satisfaction in him. Augustine, the great father of the church, expressed this most beautifully when he said: "Lord God, you have made all things for yourself, and our hearts are restless until they find their rest in you." May God grant us all to know this rest, may he draw us into his solitude and silence. We will thank him for it.

✳

ON PSALM 42

Sermon for the 6th Sunday After Easter, June 2, 1935

This sermon is found in the collection of sermons from Finkenwalde. It was reproduced and distributed by the seminary as an aid to meditation. In it, we see how closely Bonhoeffer now keeps to the biblical text, moving from word to word in his meditations.

Psalm 42 was a childhood favorite of his. At age fourteen he composed a cantata on the sixth verse: "Why are you so full of heaviness, O my soul?"[23]

Editorial notes: (1) After the brief prayers that conclude the commentary on each psalm verse, there follows in the original a verse of some familiar Lutheran hymn. (2) At verse 7 in the German Bible text we read, "He helps me with his countenance," which sounds strange to us but not to Bonhoeffer. For him Christ is God's countenance. (3) I have used the feminine pronoun throughout, which Bonhoeffer did not do.

Psalm 42

1   As the deer longs for the water-brooks,
     so longs my soul for you, O God.

Have you heard the bellowing of a hart penetrating a
cold autumn night in the forest? The whole forest
trembles under its longing cry. Here a human soul
cries out, not for some earthly good, but for God. A
devout person, from whom God is far removed, longs
for the God of grace and salvation. She knows the God
to whom she cries. She is not the seeker after the
unknown God who will never find anything. She once
experienced God's help and nearness. Therefore, she
does not call into the void. She calls for her God. We
can only rightly seek God when God has already
revealed himself to us, when we have found him
before.

*Lord God, awaken in my soul a great longing for
you. You know me and I know you. Help me to
seek you and find you. Amen.*

2   My soul is athirst for God, athirst for
     the living God;
    when shall I come to appear before the
     presence of God?

Thirst for God. We know the body's thirst when there
is no water; we know the thirst of our passion for life
and good fortune. Do we also know the soul's thirst
for God? A God who is only an ideal can never still
this thirst. Our soul thirsts for the living God, the God
and Source of all true life. When will God quench our

thirst? When will we come to appear before his presence? To be with God is the goal of all life and is itself eternal life. We are in God's presence with Jesus Christ, the crucified. If we have found God's presence here, then we thirst to enjoy it completely in eternity.

Jesus says that whoever is thirsty should come to him and drink (Jn. 7:37).

Lord, we long to come more and more into your presence. Amen.

3   My tears have been my food day and night,
      while all day long they say to me, "Where
        now is your God?"

Where is your God? People ask us that question in a doubting or mocking way. Death and sin, want and war, as well as bravery, power, and honor—that is what people see. But where is your God? We need not be ashamed of the tears we shed because we do not yet see God, because we cannot demonstrate God's presence to our sisters and brothers. Those are tears that flow for God's sake and that he records in his book (Ps. 56:8). Where is your God? What can we answer? We can only point to the person who in life, death, and resurrection proved himself to be God's true son. In death he is our life, in sin our forgiveness, in distress our helper, in war our peace. "You shall point to this person and say: that is God" (Luther).

Lord Jesus, when I am tempted, because I cannot see God and his power and love in this world, let me firmly look upon you, for you are my Lord and my God. Amen.

4   I pour out my soul when I think on these
       things:
      how I went with the multitude and led them
      into the house of God,
5   With the voice of praise and thanksgiving,
      among those who keep holy-day.

I am alone. There is no one here to whom I can pour out my soul. So I do it by myself and before the God to whom I cry. It is good when one is alone to pour out one's soul and not to be eaten up by care. But the lonelier I am the greater will be my longing for the fellowship of other Christians, for common worship, common prayer and song, praise, thanksgiving, and celebration. I remember them and my love for them grows within me. In calling for my God I call for Jesus Christ. In calling for Jesus Christ I call for the church.

God, Holy Ghost, give me brothers and sisters with whom I can have fellowship in faith and prayer, with whom I can bear everything that is laid upon me. Lead me back into your church, to your Word and to the Holy Communion. Amen.

6   Why are you so full of heaviness, O my soul?
      and why are you so disquieted within me?
7   Put your trust in God;
      for I will yet give thanks to him,
      who is the help of my countenance, and
        my God.

Heaviness and disquietude last only a short time. They should not take possession of my soul. Speak to your own soul; do not allow it to torment you and cause you grief. Say to it: Put your trust in God! Do not put your trust in sudden good fortune, but trust in

God. Jesus Christ, who is God's countenance, will certainly be my helper, and I will surely thank him for it. *Triune God, make my heart firm and let it be grounded only upon you and your help. Then I will be helped indeed, and I will thank you forever. Amen.*

8   My soul is heavy within me;
        therefore I will remember you from the
            land of Jordan,
        and from the peak of Mizar among the
            heights of Hermon.

Why this regression? Must comfort always be followed by sadness? That is the way with the human heart; it does not want to let itself be comforted, but falls from one grief to the next, and can only be held firm by God. Far from the temple in Jerusalem, far from the church and the congregation of the faithful, the longing remains sharp and unstilled. The heart remembers God, and the mind thinks of the spiritual home in which there will be peace and joy. When will I see it again?

Father, when you send me into an alien land, then may I be sustained by that healthy longing for my spiritual home, and may you direct my thoughts to the eternal homeland in which you will comfort us. Amen.

9   One deep calls to another in the noise
        of your cataracts;
        all your rapids and floods have gone over me.

Deeps, cataracts, rapids, and floods—do you hear how the sea of the world crashes over the devout person? It wants to swallow her up; she is like a drowning woman, who can find no solid ground and whose strength is failing. That is how the world gains its power over us. Do we know the one whom the wind and the sea obey, who rises up and rebukes the sea and makes it still? (Mt. 8:23-27).

Lord Jesus Christ, do not let me sink! Speak your strong word and save me! You alone can help. Amen.

10　The LORD grants his loving-kindness in
　　　　the daytime;
　　　in the night season his song is with me,
　　　　a prayer to the God of my life.

Day and night, how endlessly long and comfortless they are when we are without God. But how happy the worst day becomes when I hold fast to God's goodness and believe, when I know that all things work together for good to those who love God. And how still and liberating does the deepest night become when I sing and pray to God, to the God who desires not my death but my life, to the God of my life. God's promises are true and they fill day and night, week by week, year by year. If I only hold on to them!

God, Holy Ghost, fulfill all your promises in me. I am ready day and night. Fill me completely. Amen.

11　I will say to the God of my strength, "Why
　　　　have you forgotten me?
　　　and why do I go so heavily while the enemy
　　　　oppresses me?"

Why have you forgotten me? Every Christian asks this question at some time, when everything is going against her, when all earthly hope is smashed, when she feels completely lost in the course of great world events, when all of life's goals collapse and everything seems to lack sense. But what matters then is who she is questioning. Not an obscure fate, but "the God of my strength," the eternal source on which my life depends. I go heavily in my doubt, but God remains the source of strength; I sway, God stands immovable; I become false, God remains true—"the God of my strength."

Lord, my God, be my strong deliverer, to whom I can turn now and always. Amen.

12 While my bones are being broken,
    my enemies mock me to my face;
13 All day long they mock me
    and say to me, "Where now is your God?"

Over the centuries the devout have endured mockery and been made a laughing-stock for the sake of the faith. It is deeply painful when not a day goes by without the name of God being called in doubt and blasphemed. Where now is your God? I confess God before the world and all his enemies when, in the deepest distress, I believe in God's goodness; when, in guilt, I believe in his forgiveness; in death, life; in defeat, victory; in abandonment, God's gracious presence. Whoever has found God in the cross of Jesus Christ knows how mysteriously God hides himself in this world and how, when we believe him farthest away, he is just there beside us. Whoever has found God in the cross forgives all her enemies because God has forgiven her.

*God, forsake me not when I have to suffer shame
and disgrace; forgive all the godless people because
you have forgiven me, and bring us all finally by
the cross of your dear Son to you. Amen.*

14 Why are you so full of heaviness, O my soul?
 and why are you so disquieted within me?
15 Put your trust in God;
 for I will yet give thanks to him,
 who is the help of my countenance, and
  my God.

Now, be rid of all your care, and wait! God knows the
hour of help, and it will come just as surely as God is
God. He will be the help of your countenance;
because he knows you and loved you before he made
you. He will not let you fall. You are in his hands. At
the end you will only be able to thank him for everything that has happened to you, because through it all
you will have learned that the almighty God is your
God. Your salvation is in Jesus Christ.

 *Triune God, I thank you that you have chosen me
and loved me. I thank you for every way in which
you lead me. I thank you that you are my God.
Amen.*

*

ON PSALM 50:1-6

A Sermon Outline for Advent

1935 was the first year of operation for the seminary at Finkenwalde. During this year, Bonhoeffer delivered his lectures on the cost of discipleship to the seminarians. By the season of Advent it had become clear that the Nazi regime was not going to tolerate the Confessing Church. On December 2 a law was passed denying groups or associations within the state church power to collect funds, examine, or ordain. One ordinand wrote in a letter to friends on December 8, 1935: "Everything we do here is now illegal and contrary to the law of the state." Bethge comments: "The Protestant Church was not in the habit of opposing state legislation, but from 1935 onwards it was becoming increasingly clear that resistance would have to be offered."

This psalm of God's judgment of his people would have been read and heard in the context of the judgment of the church in Germany that was then taking place. The text from 1 Peter concerning God's judgment beginning with his own household (the church) was often quoted by Bonhoeffer, as it is in this sermon outline.[24]

Editorial note: The word that I translate "loving-kindness" throughout is the German word freund-lichkeit—*friendliness or kindness.*

Psalm 50

1   The LORD, the God of gods, has spoken;
      he has called the earth from the rising of the
         sun to its setting.

God speaks and calls the earth ever since he spoke on the first day of creation. He continues to command his creation. Thus he shows his love of what he has created through his word and his commandment.

2   Out of Zion, perfect in its beauty,
      God reveals himself in glory.

But where do you recognize him in the midst of the terrors of nature? Where will you read off his name? You must admit that the created order remains dumb. God indeed speaks to the world, but not to you. To you he comes from another place: Zion! Here alone does he allow you to see his loving-kindness and his glory. Here his appearance is like the glory of the morning after the night is past. In Zion, in the place where he has chosen to dwell, in the place of his promise and his faithfulness, here has the Creator manifested himself. In his grace and mercy he reveals his glory, in his loving-kindness his beauty.

3   Our God will come and will not keep silence;
before him there is a consuming flame,
and round about him a raging storm.

In this bright glory the creator God is our God. He who calls the world comes out of Zion as our God. He shows himself to be our God in that he does not keep silence, but speaks to us. He does not speak to nature like this. God's speech, coming to us out of Zion, is the glory that shines forth from Bethlehem.

4   He calls the heavens and the earth from above
to witness the judgment of his people.

Like the whirling, threatening sword of the angel before Paradise, like Jacob having to wrestle with the angry God at Jabbok, the consuming flame goes before him here. In the same way the Baptist went before Christ. So he comes to his people and calls them to judgment. The message of Advent and Christmas is also a frightening message: "May Jesus Christ be praised.... Lord have mercy!"

Does he come to judge his people? "You alone have I known" (Amos 3:2). "The time has come for the judgment to begin; it is beginning with God's own household" (1 Peter 4:17). The lightning strikes the high trees first. But God's people will be sanctified by the judgment and the loving-kindness of the Lord. The only way into the promised land is the way that goes through the whirling sword of the angel. Only through judgment does grace appear, the glory of the forgiveness and loving-kindness of God.

5 "Gather before me my loyal followers,
　　those who have made a covenant with me
　　and sealed it with sacrifice."

The loyal followers have been sanctified through the sacrifice of the cross. Against the background of Advent, the cross comes into view. Here, in this sacrifice, God's judgment and his loving-kindness are one.

6 Let the heavens declare the rightness
　　of his cause;
　　for God himself is judge.

Just as the heavens are opened for us at Christmas and the same heavens are darkened on Good Friday, so in this psalm everything that is created must serve the community of the faithful. That is the goal. All other words of creation must serve the Word out of Zion. When God one day stands in the midst of his loyal followers, then the rightness of his cause will be openly declared by all creation. Then it will be revealed that his righteous cause was begun in Bethlehem and completed at Golgotha. Heaven and earth will then bow before him. Christ will then be revealed as judge of all the earth.

*

ON PSALM 90

A Sermon at the Funeral of Frau Julie Bonhoeffer

Dietrich Bonhoeffer preached this sermon at the funeral of his grandmother in Berlin on January 15, 1936. She was a person of strong character, as the sermon attests. In April 1933, when she was ninety-one years of age, she defied a Nazi boycott of Jewish-owned firms by walking through a cordon of brownshirts to buy strawberries from a Jewish merchant.

He preached from Psalm 90, which was always read in the Bonhoeffer home on New Year's Eve.[25]

Editorial note: The prayer book text that follows is amended at verse 3 to be in conformity with Bonhoeffer's Bible, which reads, "Come again, O child of earth."

Psalm 90

1 Lord, you have been our refuge
      from one generation to another.

2 Before the mountains were brought forth,
      or the land and the earth were born,
         from age to age you are God.

3 You turn us back to the dust and say,
      "Come again, O child of earth."

4 For a thousand years in your sight are like
         yesterday when it is past
      and like a watch in the night.

5 You sweep us away like a dream;
      we fade away suddenly like the grass.

6 In the morning it is green and flourishes;
      in the evening it is dried up and withered.

7 For we consume away in your displeasure;
      we are afraid because of your wrathful
         indignation.

8 Our iniquities you have set before you,
      and our secret sins in the light of your
         countenance.

9 When you are angry, all our days are gone;
      we bring our years to an end like a sigh.

10 The span of our life is seventy years,
      perhaps in strength even eighty,
      yet the sum of them is but labor and sorrow,
         for they pass away quickly and we
         are gone.

11 Who regards the power of your wrath?
      who rightly fears your indignation?

12 So teach us to number our days
   that we may apply our hearts to wisdom.
13 Return, O LORD; how long will you tarry?
   be gracious to your servants.
14 Satisfy us by your loving-kindness in the
      morning;
   so shall we rejoice and be glad all the days
      of our life.
15 Make us glad by the measure of the days
      that you afflicted us
   and the years in which we suffered adversity.
16 Show your servants your works
   and your splendor to their children.
17 May the graciousness of the LORD our God be
      upon us;
   prosper the work of our hands;
   prosper our handiwork.

It is with great thankfulness that we stand today at the grave of our grandmother who has departed this life. God has been very good to us in allowing her to be with us until now. We can no longer think about our own lives without thinking of hers. She belongs entirely to us and will always do so. And God has been very good to her, even to the end of her life. He did not leave her solitary. He allowed her to see children, grandchildren, and great-grandchildren. Even in the midst of her final severe illness, he gave her a few days of health and happiness so that she could celebrate Christmas Eve once more with the whole household, as she had in all the years before. With great clarity and love, she was able until the end to share in what concerned each of us personally and professionally.

She asked after everyone who was near to her and had good and loving thoughts and wishes for each one. God also enabled her to see clearly her own circumstances and gave her the strength to accept them. And while we are sad today that she is no longer with us, we should never forget how thankful we ought to be.

"Lord, you have been our refuge from one generation to another." In a life as long as hers, there are times when one learns in a special way that one needs a refuge. She lost her father early in her life, she had to give up two sons in their childhood, three grandsons fell in time of war. In her old age it became quieter around her when Grandfather died, when her brothers and sisters passed away, when finally, only a few years before her own death, our good Uncle Otto, her oldest son, was taken from us. God often visibly intervened in her life; so she had to learn again and again what she had known from childhood: "Lord, you have been our refuge from one generation to another. Before the mountains were brought forth, or the land and the earth were born, from age to age you are God."

To this she held fast in her sickness, too: resigning herself to the will of God, bearing what was laid upon her, looking steadily and clearly at reality, doing whatever was required, quietly and without complaint, accepting what could not be helped. And, in all this, she displayed great inner happiness and powerful affirmation of life. That is how she conceived her life and lived it, that is how she died, how we knew her and loved her.

"You turn us back to the dust and say, 'Come again, O child of earth.'" She was privileged to see this "coming again" in three generations, and that was the greatest joy in life for her. She always had time for her children, grandchildren, and great-grandchildren. She was there for each one with her peace and good counsel. And although she lived through the particulars of each situation with us, her judgment and counsel always possessed a great objectivity, which drew upon her unmatched knowledge of everything human and upon her great love. And as she saw the generations come and grow up, she prepared herself to go. In all her experience and wisdom, one sensed the humble recognition of the limits to all human knowledge, judgments, and life itself. "For a thousand years in your sight are like yesterday when it is past and like a watch in the night."

"The span of our life is seventy years, perhaps in strength even eighty, yet the sum of them is but labor and sorrow, for they pass away quickly and we are gone." She was ninety-three years old, and she transmitted to us the heritage of another age. With her passing a world passes, which we all in some way carry within us and want to keep within us. The inviolability of justice, the free word of a free person, the binding character of one's word, clarity and sobriety in speech, uprightness, and simplicity in both personal and public life—her whole life was stayed upon those values. They defined her life. Experience had taught her that it required work and effort to realize such goals for oneself. She never shied from that work and effort. She could not bear it when she saw those values scorned, when she saw the rights of a human being violated. Therefore her last years were burdened by her great sorrow because of the fate of the Jews among our people; she bore it with them and suffered for them. She came from another time, from another age of the spirit—and that age does *not* pass with her into the grave. That heritage, for which we thank her, is binding upon us today.

"So teach us to number our days that we may apply our hearts to wisdom." We can learn not only from her life but from her death. Even a life as fully conscious and wise as hers remains under the law of death, which governs everything human. We too must go one day, with all our ideals, our values, and our work. Applying our hearts to wisdom means knowing the limit of our life, but, even more, knowing that beyond that limit is the God who is from eternity to eternity, into whose hands we fall, whether we choose to or not, in whose hands she is now lifted up in eternity.

What ought we to say further about such a full and rich life? We call upon God, who is our refuge, to whom we can flee in all grief and sadness, Jesus Christ, in whom is all truth, all righteousness, all freedom and all love. We call upon the God who has overcome all hatred, lovelessness, and discontent through his invincible love in the cross of Jesus Christ. We ask him that she may see in eternity what is covered and buried here beneath sin and death, that she may see in all clearness and peace the eternal countenance of God in Jesus Christ.

The beginning, the end, O Lord, they are thine;
The span in between is the life that was mine;
If I stumbled in darkness, not finding my way,
In thy house is brightness, as clear as the day.

And now we will not be sorrowful anymore. That was not her way. She never wanted to make anyone sad. We must return to our work and to our daily lives. That is the way she intended it. Above all else, she loved the deed and the day's work. We want to go forth from her grave strengthened by her life and death, strengthened much more by faith in the God who was her refuge and continues to be ours, strengthened by Jesus Christ. "May the graciousness of the LORD our God be upon us; prosper the work of our hands; prosper our handiwork." Amen.

*

ON PSALM 58

A Sermon on a Psalm of Vengeance

This sermon is dated July 11, 1937 in the collected works. 1937 was the year in which the Gestapo net tightened around the Confessing Church. "By the end of 1937, 804 members of the Confessing Church had been imprisoned for longer or shorter periods." Pastor Martin Niemoeller was imprisoned by the Nazis on July 1, 1937. He would not return home for eight years. Bonhoeffer had gone to visit his colleague in the church resistance movement on the day of his arrest, not knowing what had transpired. The Gestapo found him there and placed him under house arrest, during which he witnessed the search of Niemoeller's home. "In July 1937 the wave of persecution began to engulf former Finkenwaldians. Letters spoke of interrogations, house searches, confiscations and arrests." A mother wrote to her son at the seminary in Finkenwalde after visiting one of his friends in prison: "'Evangelical Pastor' is written in large letters above the cell door. Every day they are allowed half an hour in the fresh air....He is suffering." On September 28, 1937 the Gestapo sealed the doors of the seminary at Finkenwalde. In a letter written at the end of this year, Bonhoeffer referred to these "increasingly impatient attacks by the forces of the Antichrist."

The sermon on Psalm 58 arose in this context. It can be seen as an attempt to pronounce the judgment of God on the Nazi regime, while still holding Christians back from any direct role as agents of that judgment. Two more years would elapse before Bonhoeffer joined the underground resistance.[26]

Editorial notes: Verses 1 and 7b are presented as they appear in the German Bible text. Verses 7 and 8 are in the indicative in German and in the imperative in the prayer book, but I do not think the meaning is much affected.

Psalm 58

1 Are you then dumb, that you will not speak
what is right,
and judge the children of men with equity?

2 No; you devise evil in your hearts,
and your hands deal out violence in the land.

3 The wicked are perverse from the womb;
liars go astray from their birth.

4 They are as venomous as a serpent,
they are like the deaf adder which stops
its ears,

5 Which does not heed the voice of the charmer,
no matter how skillful his charming.

6 O God, break their teeth in their mouths;
   pull the fangs of the young lions, O LORD.
7 Let them vanish like water that runs off;
   let the arrows they aim break in two.
8 Let them be like the snail that melts away,
   like a stillborn child that never sees the sun.
9 Before they bear fruit, let them be cut down
      like a brier;
   like thorns and thistles let them be swept
      away.
10 The righteous will be glad when they see
      the vengeance;
   they will bathe their feet in the blood
      of the wicked.
11 And they will say, "Surely, there is a reward
      for the righteous;
   surely, there is a God who rules in the earth."

Is this fearful psalm of vengeance to be our prayer? May we pray in this way? Certainly not! We bear much guilt of our own for the action of any enemies who cause us suffering. We must confess the righteous punishment of God in that which afflicts and humbles us sinful human beings. Even in these times of distress for the church, we must confess that God himself has raised his hand in wrath against us, in order to visit our sins upon us: our spiritual indolence, our open or hidden disobedience, our great lack of discipline in daily living under his Word. Or would we deny that every personal sin, even the most hidden one, must bring down God's wrath upon his congregation? How then should we, who are guilty ourselves and deserving of God's wrath, call down God's vengeance upon our enemies? Will not this vengeance much more strike us? No, *we* cannot pray this psalm. Not because we are too good for it (what a superficial idea, what colossal pride!), but because we are too sinful, too evil for it!

Only one who is without guilt can pray in this way. This psalm of vengeance is the prayer of the innocent. David is the one who prays this psalm, although David himself is not innocent. But it pleased God to prepare in David the one who would be called David's son—Jesus Christ. Therefore, David, from whom the Christ will come, must not perish at his enemies' hands. David could never have prayed against his enemies in this way on his own behalf, in order to preserve his own life. From what we know of David, he meekly endured all the personal abuse that he suffered. But in David is Christ, and thereby also the church of God. So his enemies are the enemies of Jesus Christ and of his holy church. That is why David must not perish at his enemies' hands. Thus it is the innocence of Christ himself that prays this psalm with David—and with Christ the whole church of God. No, we sinners do not pray this song of vengeance, innocence alone prays this psalm. The innocence of Christ steps before the world and accuses it. And when Christ accuses the world of sin, are we not ourselves also among the accused?

1   Are you then dumb, that you will not speak
      what is right,
     and judge the children of men with equity?

It is an evil time when the world allows injustice to occur and keeps silent. When the oppression of the poor and afflicted cries out to heaven, and the judges and rulers of the earth keep quiet. When the persecuted congregation in its hour of need calls to God for help and to humanity for justice, and no mouth on earth is opened to support its cause. "Are you then dumb, that you will not speak what is right, and judge the children of men with equity?" It is the children of men who suffer injustice. Must that always be forgotten in such times? Hear it: human beings, God's creatures like us, experiencing pain and misery like us—it is to them you do violence. They have their happiness and hopes like you, they feel honor and shame like you, children of men who are sinners like you and need God's mercy like you, your brothers and sisters! "Are you then dumb?" Oh no, you are not dumb; one hears your voice clearly on the earth. But it is an unmerciful, a biased word that you speak. You judge not with equity, but with respect to the person.

2   No; you devise evil in your hearts,
       and your hands deal out violence in the land.
If the mouths of the rulers of the world are silent about injustice at the same time their hands are dealing out violence, how frightful are the lawless actions of these human hands, causing suffering and bodily pain. The persecuted, imprisoned, beaten congregation is made to yearn for deliverance. Let me fall into the hands of God, but not the hands of men! Christ speaks here if we can still hear it. He underwent the unjust judgment, he fell into the hands of men. It is innocence here that accuses the lawless world. But we sinners encounter only the just wrath of God. How could it be otherwise? And we are not dealing here with individ-

ual failings that are common to us all. No, what is being revealed is the mystery of godlessness itself.

3   The wicked are perverse from the womb;
    liars go astray from their birth.

Into this depth of wickedness only perfect innocence may look. We may very much want to believe that there is something we can change, something we can improve; and in countless ways we attempt to bring about here or there some change for the better. That causes us to feel renewed indignation and inner turmoil whenever another great injustice occurs. Only innocence knows that here everything must happen as it does. Innocence understands the dark mystery, that Satan has already taken hold of his own in the womb, and now, while he rages and pushes on, they must do their work. The world remains the world; Satan remains Satan. In this abyss of understanding, innocence achieves perfect peace. It must be so and it will not be otherwise.

4   They are as venomous as a serpent,
    they are like the deaf adder which stops
        its ears,
5   Which does not heed the voice of the charmer,
    no matter how skillful his charming.

In the Orient there are those who can charm snakes with their voices and so make them obey. A deaf snake, however, does not hear this voice and can escape from the charmer. The wicked are compared to such deaf snakes, who do not heed the voice of the skillful charmer. It is the voice of God they do not heed. God himself is the skillful One who by his word of grace charms and controls our hearts. With the sweet words of his love he attracts us, persuades us, takes charge of our hearts, so that we listen to him as if in a spell and yield to him our obedience. There remains, however, this great mystery, that there are those who hear and those who stop their ears so that they cannot hear. We know ourselves that there are times in which our ears are deaf. There are times when, in willful disobedience, we harden our hearts against God's will and heap up sin upon sin until at last we can hear no more. Then Satan has gained control of us. In this way Satan hardens the hearts of those who must serve him in his fight against God's kingdom and God's Word. They can hear no more, so they obey no more. And because their ears are deaf to the grace of God, so are their mouths dumb for the law of God. These are the enemies of God and of his congregation, as David, Christ, and the church know them to be.

Such awareness leads to prayer. If this is the nature of the enemy, then no human arts are of any avail to bring us peace. No human power is of any more help to overcome such an enemy. We must call upon the name of God. And now there begin in our psalm those frightful petitions before which we blanch, which we can repeat only with trembling and deep inner resistance. God is called upon to take vengeance against the enemies.

6 O God, break their teeth in their mouths;
   pull the fangs of the young lions, O LORD.
We learn here, above all else, that in the face of the enemy of God and of his church we can only pray. Our own courage, no matter how great, and all our bravery

will collapse before this enemy. We are talking about the attack of Satan. Only the one who has power over Satan, God himself, can take the matter in hand. It would be a great deal if we learned just this much: that we must earnestly pray to God in such distress. And then another lesson: whoever calls for the vengeance of God renounces thereby any vengeance of his own. Whoever wants to avenge himself still does not know with whom he is dealing; he still wants to take things into his own hands. But the one who consigns vengeance to God alone is prepared to suffer and to endure, without a thought of his own revenge, without hatred or recrimination. Such a one is gentle in spirit, peaceable, loving the enemy. For that person God's cause has become more important than his own suffering. He knows that God will win the victory. "Vengeance is mine," says the LORD; "I will repay" (Deut. 32:35).

And he will repay! But we are free from revenge and retaliation. Only the one who is entirely free from hatred and would not use his prayer to satisfy a craving for revenge can pray in purity of heart: "God, break their teeth in their mouths; pull the fangs of the young lions, O LORD!" That is to say: God, it is your business alone to determine who ought to suffer harm; it is your honor that has been offended. God, now step in and destroy your enemy, use your power, let your righteous wrath blaze forth. God is not mocked. He will hold a terrible judgment over his enemies. And whether we are frightened by the dreadful wishes of the psalm or not, God's power will be even more dreadful for those whom it is directed against. If we are afraid of the fists of human beings, how much more must we be afraid of the fists of God, which will crush the wicked for the sake of his kingdom, his name, and his honor. The Lord of the world is setting up his kingdom *(reich)*. To him belongs vengeance on his enemies.

7 Let them vanish like water that runs off;
  let the arrows they aim break in two.
8 Let them be like the snail that melts away,
  like a stillborn child that never sees the sun.
9 Before they bear fruit, let them be cut down
  like a brier;
  like thorns and thistles let them be swept
  away.

Now David breaks forth in great jubilation. He is convinced that his prayer is heard. In images that press in upon each other he sees even now, in the midst of battle and distress, the defeat of the wicked. They will "vanish like water that runs off"—quickly there will be an end to them. Just as water quickly runs off, so they will disappear. "The arrows they aim break in two"—the deadly arrows still fly, but they can no longer do any harm, they are powerless.

They are "like the snail that melts away"—so full of scorn is David with regard to his enemies. When God tramples upon the powerful and great of this earth, it will be as if he were stepping on a snail. "Like a stillborn child that never sees the sun"—it will be all over with them as fast as that, they will remain in the dark and be forgotten, and no one will ask after them. "Cut down like a brier before they bear fruit"—God's anger will not allow the plans of his enemies to come to fruition. Before their time, the wicked will be swept away with force. They will bring nothing to conclusion; that is God's punishment. It will come quickly, more quickly than we anticipate.

10 The righteous will be glad when they see
    the vengeance;
  they will bathe their feet in the blood
    of the wicked.

Once more we shudder as we read this psalm. Is it not quite impossible for us as Christians to pray for such an outcome? My dear congregation, if we avoid this we have understood nothing. This concerns God and his righteousness only. The wicked must die so that God's righteousness may triumph. This does not have to do with human friendship and human compassion. It has to do only with God maintaining the victory. Whoever shrinks from this joy in the vengeance of God and in the blood of the wicked does not yet know what took place on the cross of Christ. God's righteous vengeance on the wicked has already been achieved. The blood of the wicked has already flowed. God's judgment of death upon godless humanity has been spoken. God's righteousness is fulfilled in the cross of Christ.

Jesus Christ died the death of the godless; he was stricken by God's wrath and vengeance. His blood is the blood which God's righteousness required for the transgression of his commandments. God's vengeance has been carried out in the midst of the earth in a manner more fearful than even this psalm knows about. Christ, the innocent, died the death of the wicked, so that we need not die. Now we stand beneath his cross as the godless ones, and now a most

difficult mystery is resolved: Jesus Christ, the innocent, prays in the hour of God's vengeance on the
wicked of the earth, in which our psalm is fulfilled:
"Father, forgive them, for they know not what they do"
(Lk. 23:34). Only he who bore the vengeance could
pray for the forgiveness of the wicked; because he
alone has set us free from God's wrath and vengeance;
he has brought forgiveness to his enemies and no one
may offer this prayer but him. When we behold him,
the crucified one, we realize God's wrath against us
wicked ones. And in the same moment we experience
his deliverance from this wrath, as we hear: "Father,
forgive them, for they know not what they do."

"The righteous will be glad when they see the
vengeance; they will bathe their feet in the blood of the
wicked." Is that not genuine joy before God? Is that
not the gladness we feel because God's righteousness
has triumphed in the cross? Should not the righteous
rejoice in the victory of Christ? God's vengeance is
extinguished, and the blood of the wicked, in which we
bathe ourselves, gives us a share in God's victory; the
blood of the wicked has become our salvation, making
us clean from all sins. That is the great marvel.

So there emerges from the midst of this vengeance
psalm the picture of the bloody Savior, who died for
the godless, who was stricken by God's vengeance for
our salvation. No one is excluded here. Christ bore the
whole vengeance of God for all. Whoever comes to
him, whoever cleaves to him, will never more be
touched by the wrath and vengeance of God. That
person is in the protection of the righteousness of
Christ, whoever he may be. Whoever will not come,
whoever will not cast himself down before the cross of

Christ, whoever despises the cross, will suffer God's wrathful judgment, the vengeance of God, as it came upon Christ—but not unto life, rather unto eternal death.

11 And they will say, "Surely, there is a reward
   for the righteous;
      surely, there is a God who rules in the earth."

The reward of the righteous is not the happiness or the power or the honor of this world. It is nothing other than the fellowship of the cross of Christ, the redemption from the wrath of God. "There is a God who rules in the earth." Where can we see God's judgment upon the wicked of the earth? Not in visible misfortune, unhappiness, or shame before the world, but only in the cross of Jesus Christ. Is that not enough for us? Do we not see in the cross all the enemies of God already defeated and condemned? What is the good of all our discontent, which wants to see more than this judgment of God? Therefore, when we come to doubt God's righteousness upon earth, let us look upon the cross of Christ: there is judgment, there is pardon.

The deliverance of the righteous and the damnation of the wicked, as we will finally see it on the day of judgment, is concealed from us today by the Crucified One in his love. We could not bear it upon this earth. But we can be certain that everything will serve to make the righteous glad. The victory and triumph of Christ will be revealed in deliverance and judgment. But until that day, Satan will push on the enemies in their attack against Christ and his congregation, with injustice and deeds of violence. In the midst of this storm, Christ prays this psalm as our representative. He accuses the wicked, he calls down upon them God's vengeance and his righteousness, and he gives himself for all the wicked in his innocent suffering on the cross.

And now we too pray this psalm with him, in humble thanks that we have been granted deliverance from wrath through the cross of Christ; in the fervent plea that God will bring all of our enemies under the cross of Christ and grant them grace; in the burning desire that the day may soon come in which Christ visibly triumphs over his enemies and establishes his kingdom. Thus have we learned to pray this psalm. Amen.

＊

ON PSALM 34:19

A Sermon on the Suffering of the Righteous

*This meditation was sent from Tegel Prison on June 8,
1944, along with a brief letter to Eberhard Bethge and his
wife, Renate. Bonhoeffer had been imprisoned in April
1943, following the attempts on Hitler's life in March of
that year. In June 1944 he was still awaiting a trial date
and had some hope that he might see his friends again.
The failure of the next assassination attempt on July 20,
1944, and the subsequent discovery of information about
the circle of military officers involved in planning it,
would remove that hope.*

*Bonhoeffer had become engaged to marry Maria von
Wedemeyer only a few months before his arrest and
imprisonment, and his separation from her added another
dimension of suffering to his life.*

*The two Scripture verses on which this meditation is
based are Bible portions from the* Herrnhuter
Losungen. *Published yearly since 1732, the* Losungen
was a collection of brief texts intended for daily medita-

tion throughout the year, and Bonhoeffer seems to have meditated on them regularly. He sometimes sought direction from them for his decisions. The decision to leave the safety of America, where he had been invited to lecture, and return to Germany in the summer of 1939, seemed to find confirmation for him in the Losung *text for June 26 of that year: "Do your best to come before winter" (2 Tim. 4:21). He wrote about the text: "That follows me around all day. It is as if we were soldiers home on leave, and going back into action.... 'Do your best to come before winter'—it is not a misuse of Scripture if I apply that to myself."*

On the sea voyage back to Germany Bonhoeffer wrote, "Since I have been on board, the inward disharmony about the future has ceased, and I can think without any reproaches about the shortened time in America. Losung: *'It is good for me that I have been afflicted, that I might learn your statutes' (Ps. 119:71). One of my favorite passages from my favorite psalm."[27]*

Editorial notes: (1) The two Scripture verses are translated directly from the German. (2) The Latin word sensorium *may be translated "consciousness" or "seat of sensation." (3) I have alternated masculine and feminine pronouns.*

Psalm 34

19 The righteous person must suffer many things; but the Lord delivers him out of them all.

1 Peter 3:9

> Repay not evil with evil or railing with railing,
> but rather bless, and know that you are called to
> this, so that you should inherit the blessing.

The righteous person suffers in this world in a way
that the unrighteous person does not. The righteous
persons suffers because of many things that for others
seem only natural and unavoidable. The righteous
person suffers because of unrighteousness, because of
the senselessness and absurdity of events in the world.
She suffers because of the destruction of the divine
order of marriage and the family. She suffers not only
because it means privation for her, but because she
recognizes something ungodly in it. The world says:
That is how it is, always will be, and must be. The
righteous person says: It ought not to be so; it is
against God. This is how one recognizes the righteous
person, by her suffering in just this way. She brings, as
it were, the *sensorium* of God into the world; hence,
she suffers as God suffers in this world.

"But the Lord delivers him." God's deliverance is
not to be found in every experience of human suffering. But in the suffering of the righteous God's help is
always there, because he is suffering with God. God is
always present with him. The righteous person knows
that God allows him to suffer so, in order that he may
learn to love God for God's own sake. In suffering, the
righteous person finds God. That is his deliverance.
Find God in your separation and you will find deliverance!

The answer of the righteous person to the sufferings that the world causes her is to bless. That was the

answer of God to the world that nailed Christ to the cross: blessing. God does not repay like with like, and neither should the righteous person. No condemning, no railing, but blessing. The world would have no hope if this were not so. The world lives and has its future by means of the blessing of God and of the righteous person. Blessing means laying one's hands upon something and saying: You belong to God in spite of all. It is in this way that we respond to the world that causes us such suffering. We do not forsake it, cast it out, despise or condemn it. Instead, we recall it to God, we give it hope, we lay our hands upon it and say: God's blessing come upon you; may God renew you; be blessed, you dear God-created world, for you belong to your creator and redeemer. We have received God's blessing in our happiness and in our suffering. And whoever has been blessed herself cannot help but pass this blessing on to the next one; yes, wherever she is, she must be herself a blessing. The renewal of the world, which seems so impossible, becomes possible in the blessing of God.

As Jesus ascended to heaven, "he lifted up his hands and blessed" his followers. We hear him speak to us in this hour: "The Lord bless you and keep you. The Lord make his face to shine upon you and be gracious unto you. The Lord lift up his countenance upon you and give you peace." Amen.

III

MEDITATION ON PSALM 119

MEDITATION ON PSALM 119

This meditation is dated 1939/40 in the collected works. During this period Bonhoeffer was once again teaching ordinands, first in an old vicarage at Gross Schlonwitz and then in a farmstead at Sigurdshof in Pomerania. In these out-of-the-way places community life like that at Finkenwalde was briefly restored. One of the seminarians—Gerhard Lehne, whose death is noted in the letter "Fallen in Action"—described this community as a "brotherhood under the Word, irrespective of the person," with an "open-mindedness and love for everything that still makes this fallen creation lovable—music, literature, sport, and the beauty of the earth—a grand way of life."

This joy in living is reflected in the "Meditation on Psalm 119." But we also find here the seriousness with which Bonhoeffer now faces his decision to join the political resistance movement. On verse 19 he writes that he knows he should not "stay aloof and refuse to participate" in earthly tasks. Commenting on verse 1, he looks at the possibility of his own death in the struggle.

*It was during this period that he traveled to New York,
where he might have taken refuge, but then returned
instead to Sigurdshof. Because of travels and other duties
Bonhoeffer was only able to begin this meditation on his
favorite psalm. It breaks off as he is commenting on verse
21; I print verses 22-24 by themselves to conclude this collection. The remainder of his short life would provide the
commentary on them.*

*At the outset of this meditation Bonhoeffer is very con-
cerned to distinguish between what he calls God's beginning and our own beginnings. It may help the reader to
know that he was very critical of Christian movements
which emphasized "conversion" in a way that led people
to stay focused on their own "beginnings." The Oxford
Group (later Moral Rearmament) came in for strong
criticism along these lines. Bethge writes: "He held that
they had replaced the witness of the gospel with the witness of personal change." He was also ready to criticize
any form of piety in his own tradition that led to preoccupation with the self. "But for goodness sake, let's turn
our eyes away from ourselves!" he once wrote to Bethge.[28]*

*Editorial notes: (1) In this meditation I have stayed
with* The Book of Common Prayer *psalm text throughout, although this has meant losing some of the commentary at verse 11 where the German is much closer to the*
King James Version: *"Thy word have I hid in mine
heart." Bonhoeffer begins his commentary here with a
reference to Luke 8:11ff., the parable of the sower, and
develops the image of the Word as a seed that wants to be
hidden or buried in us as in a fruitful plot of earth. (2)
His quotation of Psalm 16:7 is given in the older prayer
book version because it preserves the image of the lot*

being cast. (3) I have alternated masculine and feminine pronouns by verses.

Psalm 119

1 Happy are they whose way is blameless,
 who walk in the law of the LORD!

Anyone who speaks like this assumes that the beginning has been made. He lets it be understood that life with God is not essentially a matter of ever-new beginnings. That is why he calls this life walking in the law of the LORD. He recognizes that the beginning has been made, he accepts its validity, he does not want to go back behind it anymore. Because of the beginning God has made with us, our life with God is a way that will proceed in his law. Does that mean bondage for us under the law? No, it means freedom from the killing law of ceaseless beginnings. To wait from one day to the next for the new beginning, to think that one has found it countless times only to lose it again by evening—that amounts to total destruction of faith in the God who has established the beginning in his forgiving and renewing Word, in Jesus Christ, that is, in my baptism, my rebirth, my conversion.

God has once and for all converted me to himself; it is not that I have once for all converted myself to God. God has made the beginning; that is the happy certainty of faith. Therefore, it is not for me to attempt to place countless beginnings of my own next to the one beginning of God. I have been set free from that, since God's beginning lies forever behind me.

Members of the community of faith have no need to exhort one another to make a new beginning; instead, they speak to each other as those to whom God's new beginning is continuously being given. They know they are together on the way, which begins with God having found his own and which can only end with God searching for them again (v. 176).

The way between this beginning and this end is their walk in the law of the LORD. It is life lived under the Word of God in all its many shapes and forms, its richness, its inexhaustible wealth of knowledge and experience. There is really only one danger on this way, and that is to want to go behind the beginning, or, what amounts to the same thing, to lose sight of the goal. The moment that happens, the way ceases to be a way of grace and faith. It ceases to be God's own way.

So we are addressed as those who are on the way with the psalmist. The question whether it is true, whether the right beginning has really been made for us, is in principle not asked anymore, because that question causes only fruitless fear. We are to learn to understand ourselves now as those who have been placed on the way and no longer can do anything other than walk in it. There is good reason, therefore, to say nothing about the beginning, but to completely assume it as given, foreclosing all discussion, and just so, decisively laying claim to us by this beginning. Anyone who does not cease seeking after new beginnings is under the law, will be exhausted and killed by it. Anyone who proceeds from the beginning that has been given is in the law of the Lord and will be kept and preserved by it so that he may live. It is now quite understandable that our psalm should begin with a blessing on those who accept what God has done for them, who no longer live in opposition to God's action but are carried by this action, made secure in it, who walk "in the law." The praise, however, is not for us human beings, but only for the law of the Lord, in which we can come to such blessedness.

What is this "law"?

> When your son asks you in time to come, "What is the meaning of the testimonies and the statutes and the ordinances which the LORD our God has commanded you?" then you shall say to your son, "We were Pharaoh's slaves in Egypt; . . . and the LORD showed signs and wonders, great and grievous, against Egypt and against Pharaoh and all his household, before our eyes; and he brought us out from there, that he might bring us in and give us the land which he swore to give to our fathers. And the LORD commanded us to do all these statutes, to fear the LORD our God, for our good always, that he might preserve us alive, as at this day. And it will be righteousness for us, if we are careful to do all this commandment before the LORD our God, as he has commanded us." (Deut. 6:20-25)

That is the answer to the question about the law: God's deeds of deliverance, God's commandments, and God's promise. No one understands the law of God who does not know about the deliverance that has happened and the promise of what is to come. The one who asks about the law is reminded about Jesus Christ and the deliverance of human beings from the bondage of sin and death that has been completed in him, reminded of the new beginning that God has made for all people in Jesus Christ. In answer to the question about the law of God we are not presented with moral teaching or an ethical norm, instead, we hear about a completed action of God. If we ask how we should begin life with God, the Scripture answers that God has long since begun life with us. If we ask what we can do for God, we hear what God has done for us. If we ask how we can live without sin before God, the forgiveness of all sins in Jesus Christ is announced to us. If we direct our glance forward to our future deeds, God's Word calls us back to the past and says: Remember! (Deut. 7:18; 8:2; 32:7ff.). Only when we acknowledge that the decision has already taken place, the beginning has already been made, the deed already done, and done by God; only when we are met by the decision, the beginning, God's deed, and know that we are drawn into it can we hear the commandment of God as the law of life for those for whom God long since has done everything and who now are "in the law."

God's law cannot be separated from his act of deliverance. The God of the ten commandments is the God who led you out of the land of Egypt (Ex. 20:2). God gives his law to those whom he loves, those whom he has chosen and taken to himself (Deut. 7:7-11). To know God's law is grace and joy (Deut. 4:6-10). It is the way of life for those who accept God's grace (Lev. 18:5). "Yea, he loved his people; all those consecrated to him were in his hand; so they followed in thy steps, receiving direction from thee" (Deut. 33:3).

Torah, the law, originally meant that which was determined by casting lots. It is the judgment of God, which is sought at the point where human striving is at an end and where God alone must act and decide. Torah is God's cast of the lots over humanity. It goes beyond all human thought and expectation. "The lot is fallen unto me in a fair ground; yea, I have a goodly heritage" (Ps. 16:7). God's judgment is grace and life for human beings; it is life before God and with God through the forgiveness of sins.

Therefore, "happy are they who walk in the law of the LORD." They are the ones who have dared to accept God's act as having been done for them, the ones who proceed on the basis of the beginning that God has made. They are like victors after the battle is won. They are like those who have gone through the valley of death but still live. They are like those who find their way again at sunrise after a dark night of wandering. Now they press forward to a new future, now they go from victory to victory, now they are on their way in the light of day.

Happy are they, for they have been freed from the torment of their own beginnings; happy are they, because they have overcome the inner divisions that result when we oppose our own beginnings to the beginning of God; they are complete, whole, undivided, blameless. Luther calls them "completely sound" *(die ganz Gesunden)* in his first translation of the psalm in 1521. He rightly recalls the use of the word "blameless" by Paul in the pastoral epistles, "which refers to those who are without a flaw, who do not patch themselves with other teachings of men." Happy are they, for the law of their own decision is taken from them; they live in the law of the LORD.

Happy are they—these words speak of the happiness and blessedness of life in the law of the LORD. It is God's will that it should go well for those who walk in his commandments. It is no sign of a strong, mature faith if these words cause us embarrassment—if we say that God has more important things in mind than to be concerned about our well-being. ("This day you have become the people of the LORD your God" [Deut. 27:9].) There are Christians who want to be more spiritual than God himself. They like to talk of battle, renunciation, suffering, and the cross, and it is almost painful for them that the Holy Scripture speaks not only of that, but time and again of the good fortune of the devout, the well-being of the just. These Christians say that is in the Old Testament and has been superseded. But the real reason for their embarrassment is that their hearts are too constricted to be able to conceive of the great kindness of God, too narrow to be able to honor God for all the earthly gifts that he shares with those who live in his law. They want to be schoolmasters to the Holy Spirit, and so they lose the full joy of their Christian calling and deny God the thanks they should give for his great friendliness toward us.

If our psalm promises well-being, good fortune, and blessedness to those who live in God's law, we should take that quite literally. And we certainly ought to refer it to our life on earth. Or is it not true? Do devout men and women want to deny that it goes well for them here on earth (Ps. 37:36), that they lead a life full of great happiness (Ps. 37:24), that they lack nothing that is good (Ps. 34:10), that they enjoy prosperity (Ps. 34:12), yes, that the Lord gives them what their heart desires (Ps. 37:4)? "'Did you lack anything?' [Jesus asked his disciples]. They said, 'Nothing'" (Lk. 22:35). It is true that the only one who can speak this way is one who is willing to be content with God's gifts as they come, as long as they simply sustain life. Only contented hearts always experience well-being. "But if we have food and clothing, with these we shall be content" (1 Tim. 6:8).

It is surprising to observe the praise of God's kindness in providing for our well-being breaking forth with special strength in the very psalms that complain about the oppression and sufferings of the righteous. The one who prays our psalm knew misery and temptation as well. But should not the devout person who is in trouble be especially able to give thanks for all previous care and protection and for each gift that still remains to that hour? For "the little that the righteous has is better than great riches of the wicked" (Ps. 37:17). Should not such a person best understand this, knowing that we would have earned nothing but wrath and punishment if God had wanted to deal with us according to our merits?

"Blessed are you," says Jesus—and the word for blessed and happy in Hebrew is the same word. Not blessed because you lack nothing, but because you receive everything you have from the hand of God. "Be still before the LORD and wait patiently for him" (Ps. 37:7). With thanksgiving you may eat the daily bread that God has provided for those "who believe and know the truth" (1 Tim. 4:3). You know that the good gifts of creation exist for your sake so that you may live thankfully, confessing Christ and proclaiming him as the Lord of the world. You also experience daily the truth of Jesus' word that everyone who leaves house or brother or sister or father or mother or children or position for the sake of the gospel receives it all again a hundredfold "in this life" in the fellowship of the community of the faithful, and will receive "eternal life in the age to come" (Mk. 10:29ff.). So you know and confess that the loving-kindness of God is "better than life itself" (Ps. 63:3). You give thanks in your heart for all good gifts, but your heart belongs only to the Giver.

Yet it may be that God will give to one of his own the cup of suffering for Christ's sake, to be drunk to the dregs in the cross and death (that the judgment "begin with the household of God"—1 Pet. 4:17). For this only a few have been made worthy at any time. Should God require this of any, he will certainly so prepare their hearts beforehand that they will be the very ones who by their strong faith testify anew and with authority: "Happy are they who walk in the law of the LORD."

What is true for individuals is true also for the community, the household, the people. It will go well with the household and the people who walk in God's law (read Ps. 112!). It is the same God who gave the law who rules the world (read Ps. 19!); therefore, the earth will belong to those who live in God's law (Mt. 5:5; Ps. 37:10,12). Pride, insolence, and wrong-doing will collapse of themselves, but humility and the fear of God, decency and order, right and truth will endure—for God is "God in heaven above and on earth beneath" (Josh. 2:11).

2   Happy are they who observe his decrees
      and seek him with all their hearts!

A second blessing follows the first. The decrees are the warning signs that God has set up on the way of his people, so that they do not go astray. The Hebrew word used here is often translated "testimonies." The word first came into frequent use in the Babylonian captivity. There the people realized in the time of punishment and expiation that the commandments had been given as warnings and reminders of God, the Lord (Neh. 9:34). Now one calls the ark of the covenant the "ark of the testimony" (Ex. 25:22), the ten commandments "the tables of the testimony" (Ex. 31:18), the holy place "the tent of the testimony" (Num. 9:15) or the "tabernacle of the testimony" (Ex. 38:21). In this way they showed that all these things had no ultimate meaning in themselves, but were testimonies to God. Only those who found and honored God in the ten commandments, in the ark, in the tabernacle understood their true nature. God gives such testimonies to his people on their way so that in the time of trial they might know that in the end he will do them good (Deut. 8:16). Since God is the Lord of whom his decrees should daily remind us and to whom they should testify, no external observance of them can suffice. Not only lips and hands but the whole, undivided heart must be involved; it must be eternally seeking the One of whom the testimonies speak.

In the commandments, in acts of worship and prayers, the heart seeks after the One who has given them all. So it is not inactive and does not rest content, but continuously seeks God and his revelation—the

Word in the words, the gospel in the law. Blessed is the person who keeps the testimonies of God in this way, who seeks God from her whole heart. She is only able to seek because it has been shown her where she must seek and who she is to find, because it has been promised her that the seeking will end in finding.

3 Who never do any wrong,
    but always walk in his ways.

God's ways are the ways that he himself has gone and that we are now to go with him. God will not allow us to go on any way on which he himself has not preceded us. The way upon which he calls us to go is the way he has made and that he protects. So it is really his way.

> And the Lord went before them by day in a pillar of cloud to lead them along the way, and by night in a pillar of fire to give them light, that they might travel by day and by night; the pillar of cloud by day and the pillar of fire by night did not depart from before the people. (Ex. 13:21-22)

"Your way, O God, is holy; who is so great a god as our God? ... Your way was in the sea, and your paths in the great waters, yet your footsteps were not seen. You led your people like a flock" (Ps. 77:13, 19-20).

With God one does not arrive at a fixed position; rather, one walks along a way. One moves ahead or one is not with God. God knows the whole way; we only know the next step and the final goal. There is no stopping; every day, every hour it goes farther. Whoever sets his foot on this way finds that his life has become a journey on the road. It leads through green pastures and through the dark valley, but the Lord will always lead on the right pathway (Ps. 23) and he will not let your foot be moved (Ps. 121:3).

The whole message of salvation can be called simply "the Way" (Acts 19:9; 22:4; 24:14) or the "way of the Lord" (Acts 18:25-26). So it is clear that the gospel and the faith are not timeless ideas, but the action of God with human beings in history. Since it is a way, it cannot remain hidden from the eyes of other people. It will be apparent whether good things or evil things happen on this way. So it is not a matter of indifference whether evil is occasionally done on this way, as if one could retreat from imperfect reality to the ideal, or be satisfied simply to know the right way, to possess the right faith, even when one cannot always act in accordance with it. Those who walk in his ways *"never* do any wrong." Knowing the way and that one is on the right way does not reduce one's responsibility or guilt; it increases them.

God's children have no privilege except this: to know God's grace and his way, and to do no wrong. Or does God's Word say too much when it says they do *no* wrong? Is there a single Christian about whom that could be said? In asking that question, we have turned our eyes away from God's Word and onto ourselves, away from the strong promise of God to our own lack of strength. Thereby we immediately come under the power of sin, which does not want us to trust God's Word. If it is really *his* way on which we are going, then we certainly do "no wrong." If we imagine, however, only for a moment that God's way has become our way, then we have already fallen, and we do much that is wrong. For "every one who commits sin is guilty of lawlessness; sin is lawlessness" (1 Jn. 3:4). Do we Christians no longer sin then? Certainly, we have sinned and we do not deny it (1 Jn. 1:8f.). But after we have confessed it, our eyes need look no more upon our sins and our weak nature, but only to Christ and the Word of God, which determines our future and says: "No one born of God commits sin; for God's nature abides in him, and he cannot sin because he is born of God" (1 Jn. 3:9).

The way of God is his way to the human being, and only thus the way of the human being to him. The way is Jesus Christ (Jn. 14:6). Whoever is on this way, whoever is in Jesus Christ, does no wrong.

4   You laid down your commandments,
        that we should fully keep them.

That in this entire psalm God is addressed, and not human beings, is shown by the "you" with which the one who is praying now turns to God. Nor do the commandments stand in the center of this psalm, it is rather the One who commands. Not an "it," an idea, but a "you" meets us in the commandments. A further sign of this is found in the Hebrew word for "commandments" in this verse. It is a word that cannot be translated by a single word of ours. It derives from the verb for seeking, visiting, paying attention to. Hence, the commandments are what God looks at, pays attention to, and the means by which he seeks and visits the human being. The commandments then reflect God's way toward the human being. They have a definite purpose and goal for me. They are not given for their own sake, but for our sake, that we "should fully keep them." We ought to keep them in the sense of holding fast to them; indeed, we should do so fully, with all our might, so that we do not lose them or let them be torn away from us. God's commandment is not only here for the moment, but for the duration. It is intended to penetrate deep within us and to be held fast in all situations of life.

5 Oh, that my ways were made so direct
     that I might keep your statutes!

The sigh "Oh!" can express a minor vexation but also a nameless sorrow. At times a whole life history can only find expression in this way. When the one who is poor and miserable has to suppress her pain within herself, then this sigh arises from the soul, and when it is accompanied by eyes looking upward to the One who can help us, it has the power of a mighty prayer (J. Geyser: *Pia desideria,* 1878). The "Oh" of our wishes is not the same as the "Oh" of prayer. One proceeds from our need as we ourselves understand it, the other proceeds from our need as God has taught us to see it. The one is desperate and demanding, the other is humble and confident. Even this right kind of sigh we cannot bring forth from our own heart. God must teach us through the Holy Spirit how to utter it. When he does, then all that is inarticulate in our deepest need comes together before God. It is the sighing of the Holy Spirit, who "himself intercedes for us with sighs too deep for words" (Rom. 8:26). This sighing is not hidden from God (Ps. 38:9).

Our *wishes* direct themselves toward an improvement of the world; our *prayer* must begin with ourselves. How we yearn that human beings would be different from what they are, that the evil in the world would end and a new righteousness take its place. But we get nowhere with all of that. All repentance and renewal must begin with me. "Oh, that *my* ways were made so direct that I might keep your statutes!" That is a prayer that has promise. "The desire of the sluggard kills him for his hands refuse to labor" (Prov. 21:25). But here there is enough for every hand to do. This prayer leads straightway to action, and just where it is most needed—in what concerns myself. But clearly this action can only proceed from prayer, or else it too will be lost. "Oh, that *my* ways...." Looking upon the evil-doing of others does not help me, and it helps me just as little to marvel at the righteousness of others if my own ways are not made right, if I cannot be righteous too.

One goal must emerge from the many goals in my life, one single direction from the different directions in which I run: God's statutes. Out of the crooked and twisted a straight way shall emerge, which is not "blocked and made crooked by human doctrine" (Luther). God's statutes alone remain firm, drawn up by him for all times. Heaven, earth, and humanity have their course decreed by these statutes. As unchanging as the return of day and night is God's covenant with his people. "Thus says the LORD: If I have not established my covenant with day and night and the ordinances of heaven and earth, then I will reject the descendants of Jacob and David my servant" (Jer. 33:25-26, 31:35-36). The creation and the law are the two great unbreakable statutes of God, which eternally belong together, because the same God has given them (Ps. 19). God holds his statutes inviolate; he is faithful. Oh, that my ways were made so direct that I might enter into his faithfulness.

6   Then I should not be put to shame,
     when I regard all your commandments.

To be put to shame is the opposite of happiness. My life is ruined if that on which I relied collapses; for then I have nothing more to give my life meaning and justification, nothing more I can appeal to. My life will be ridiculed and I myself put to shame. I relied on my strength and I became weak and ill; I increased my possessions and they were taken from me overnight; I trusted in my prestige and power, then I had a great fall; I was pleased by my righteous behavior, then sin overpowered me. So everyone collapses who "makes flesh his arm" (Jer. 17:5). The world mocks one of its own merely by pointing a finger at him. Whoever comes to honor with the world will be put to shame with it.

But when I no longer regard other human beings, honor, or possessions, but God's commandments alone, then I will not be put to shame, because God's commandments cannot fail. It is God himself who holds them fast, and with them each one who has regard for them. Never will I have to be ashamed to have regarded God's commandments. Never will my life be without an advocate. Whether or not the world's judgment is against me, God will speak for me. I have regard for God's commandments when I do not allow my decisions to be determined by other people, nor by my own thoughts and experiences, but when, ever anew, even against my most devout thoughts and experiences, I ask what it is that God commands me to do. Even with my most devout decisions and ways I can come to ruin, but never with God's commandments. Not my piety but God alone preserves me from shame and destruction.

"*All* your commandments"—so varied is our life, so manifold the temptations and dangers, so new each moment, that no commandment of God is given in vain. Only the full treasure of the commandments of God can lead me securely through my life. I can be certain that there is no life situation for which God's Word will not speak the necessary direction. But it requires earnest attentiveness, tireless questioning and study in order to perceive the right commandment and thus be able to recognize the inexhaustible goodness of God in all his commandments. The more sharply the world presses against me and condemns me, the more narrow and difficult my way becomes, the more determined must be my regard for all of God's commandments. Then I will not be put to shame but will belong to those of whom it must be said: Happy are they who walk in the law of the LORD.

7   I will thank you with an unfeigned heart,
      when I have learned your righteous
         judgments.

The giving of thanks can only begin when the gift of the divine Word is acknowledged; indeed, only when I am immersed in the study of the divine Word. How could one begin to give thanks to God and not concern oneself with his Word? What kind of thanks would it be to receive the gifts but refuse the required obedience to the giver? It would be a pagan thanksgiving, which is indeed widely practiced. That is not a giving of thanks to the Lord God, but rather to an impersonal fate or fortune to which I am in no way obligated. Thanks to God that does not proceed from an obedient heart is presumption and falsehood. Only when God's revealed Word has made our heart want to obey him can we thank God for earthly and heavenly gifts.

Pagans, however, even though they receive the gifts of creation, even though they know there is a God, "do not honor him as God or give thanks to him" (Rom. 1:21). The thanksgiving of the world refers always to the self; one seeks through giving thanks only a higher confirmation and consecration of one's own good fortune (Nietzsche). By giving thanks one gains the satisfaction of feeling that the gifts received are now one's rightful possession. But there is also among the devout a way of giving thanks that is not permissible. The Pharisee thanked God and sinned (Lk. 18:9ff.) because he saw only himself in his thanksgiving; he did not receive the gifts humbly, instead he used them against his neighbor. So he could not give thanks "with an unfeigned heart" or he would have forgotten himself in giving thanks; he would not have acted like one who had something to boast of before God, but (in the manner of our psalmist) like one whose only concern is to "learn your righteous judgments." What God gave and what I was not capable of giving, God's riches toward me and my poverty toward God—these are necessarily united when I give thanks "with an unfeigned heart."

Thus the law appears to the one who gives thanks here not so much as a gift but as the "righteous judgments" of God. I thank God because I want to learn and know what he requires of me, but I thank him as one who is still only learning, who still lacks everything when measured by God's righteous judgments. So thanksgiving leads me back to the giving God and then forward to the commanding God, in order finally to find in him his righteousness, which I experience anew as righteousness given to me. "Whoever offers me the sacrifice of thanksgiving honors me; but to those who keep in my way will I show the salvation of God" (Ps. 50:24).

8   I will keep your statutes;
     do not utterly forsake me.

We must first unlearn the way in which we say "I will" before the Holy Spirit can teach us to say it in a new and right way. In matters of piety, the "I will" can cause the greatest harm: "I will be devout, I will be holy, I will keep the commandments." We must first come really to understand that even here it is not our will, but the will of God that matters. We must cancel even our devout "I" so that God can do his work in us. Otherwise the "I will" leads only to bankruptcy.

When, by the grace of God, we have stopped saying "I will," when we have been brought onto God's way by means of his new beginning with us in Jesus Christ—in spite of our "I will" and our "I will not"—then the Holy Spirit begins to speak in us, and we say in a totally new and different way: "I will." "As soon as the Holy Spirit through Word and Sacrament has begun such a work of new birth and renewal in us, it is certain that we through the power of the Holy Spirit can and should work with him, although still in great weakness" (Formula of Concord S.D. II 65). Now, as one who has been called blessed, who has cried for

God's help, who has praised and thanked God, I may say "I will"—yes, I will keep your statutes. I do this not as one compelled to do so, but as one you have set free so that I can will that which I formerly hated. Thus do you bind my will to your statutes. It is God the Holy Spirit who makes true for me what was only true for Jesus Christ, that my will is what you command. But, because I am not the Holy Spirit or the Lord Jesus Christ, I must quickly add to my "I will" the prayer: "Do not forsake me overmuch" (Luther 1521), because then it would soon be all over with my weak intentions. We are not to imagine here that God is going to take his Holy Spirit from us, for then we would have to pray: "Do not forsake me *for a moment,*" because without the Holy Spirit our good will cannot continue for a moment. It says, however, "Do not forsake me overmuch"—"not utterly"—and so we are to think of that forsaking by means of which God tests our faith, as it was said of Hezekiah: "God left him to himself, in order to try him and to know all that was in his heart" (2 Chron. 32:31).

We are to think of misfortune, misery, need of all kinds, in which God leaves us for a brief moment. We ought not to ask in our prayer that God preserve us from all misfortune, but that he might turn to us soon again, make an end of the test, and not forsake us utterly, for we are weak and we soon fail. We are only able to keep God's statutes when we are strengthened through the grace and help of God's presence. We pray for a steadfast heart that keeps itself in God's commandments, and we know that this can only be achieved by grace (Heb. 13:9).

So the circle is complete. God's grace is at the beginning; grace makes the beginning for us, so that we may be freed from our own beginnings; grace puts us on the way; and it is grace for which we pray from step to step.

Note how in these verses and in all that follow we find over and over again: *your* law, *your* commandments, *your* statutes, and so forth. Human beings are not being praised here, but God and his revelation.

9   How shall a young man cleanse his way?
     By keeping to your words.

It was a young man who prayed this psalm and this verse (cf. vv. 99-100). So this is not the question of an older person looking at the evils of youth. This question grows out of personal experiences of temptations and personal encounters with the Word of God. A young man here asks the question of his life, and he asks it not because of flaming idealism or enthusiasm for the good and noble in general, but because he has experienced the power of the Word of God and his own weakness.

Does this question about the blameless and pure way sound inconsistent with youth, freedom, and affirmation of life? If so, it is only because we have become accustomed to a very godless conception of youth and are no longer able to understand the power and fullness of life that is found in innocence. It is very presumptuous and wrongheaded to think that the human being has to become entangled deeply in the guilt of life in order to know life itself, and finally God. We do not learn to know life and guilt from our own experience, but only from God's judgment of humanity and his grace in the cross of Jesus Christ. To want to bring in sin at a particular point in one's education is a frivolous game for which a heavy price must be paid. "Remember also your Creator in the days of your youth, before the evil days come, and the years draw nigh, when you will say, 'I have no pleasure in them'" (Eccl. 12:1). "Before falling ill, humble yourself, and when you are on the point of sinning, turn back" (Sir. 18:21). "Shun youthful passions" (2 Tim. 2:22).

To be pure then, when impurity is still a danger, to be blameless not as a result of middle-class contentment, but love of God, that is no renunciation of life, rather it is life's fulfillment; it is no contempt for God's creation, rather it sanctifies creation through obedience to the Creator. "Rejoice, O young man, in your youth...; walk in the ways of your heart and the sight of your eyes. But know that for all these things God will bring you into judgment" (Eccl. 11:9). He who brings his coarse sins with him into mature adulthood will often find it too late to become their master. God is the ruler of the human being from his first breath, and he will not relinquish his rule for a moment. God does not ask about our more or less modern ideals concerning youth; he only asks whether a life has been surrendered to his rule.

In asking the question about the cleansing of his way, the young person acknowledges the sin that dwells within him. Otherwise he would not need to ask. And it is only because he knows the power of sin over his heart and his nature that he no longer looks for help by human means. Not good intentions, burning ideals, not even work and fulfillment of duty can keep the way pure, only God's Word can do that. For only God himself can deal with sin. He has done it by forgiving us all our sins in Jesus Christ (cf. Jn. 15:3); he does it by enabling us to know his Word of grace and judgment, and by leading us and giving us his grace day by day. To what shall I keep in the hour of temptation and trial? To God's Word alone. So will my way be cleansed.

10　With my whole heart I seek you;
　　　let me not stray from your commandments.

Whoever has received God's Word has to seek God; she can do no other. The more clearly and deeply God's Word shows itself to her, the more lively will be her desire for the total clarity and the unfathomable depth of God himself. Through the gift of his Word, God drives us to seek for an ever richer knowledge and a more glorious gift. He does not intend any false contentment for us. The more we receive, the more we must seek him, and the more we seek, the more we will receive from him. "To the one who has will more be given." God wants to fully glorify himself and make himself known to us in his complete richness. Of course, we can only seek God in his Word, but this Word is lively and inexhaustible, for God himself lives in it. If we are responding to God's Word we will say: I seek you with my *whole heart*. For with half a heart we might be seeking an idol, but never God himself. God requires the whole heart. He wants nothing (no thing) from us, but he wants us, and completely. His Word has told us that. Therefore, we seek him with our whole heart.

We have only one remaining concern, that we might stray from the way that has been begun for us, from the commandments we have heard. The psalmist speaks of straying; he is not thinking here of a deliberate, willful transgressing of the divine commandments. But how easily we stray when our vision is clouded by that which is evil. We wander into byways, lose our sense of direction, and cannot find our way back to the commandments of God. We must daily pray to God to keep us from the sin of straying, the unconscious sin (Num. 15:22ff.); for we at first move unconsciously onto ways that are wrong, then we often experience pleasures there, and from what was a mistake there grows an evil intention. But the one who seeks God with her whole heart will not go astray.

11   I treasure your promise in my heart,
    that I may not sin against you.

I do not treasure God's promise in my understanding but in my heart. It is not to be analysed by my intellect, but to be pondered in my heart. It is like the word of a dear friend that lives in my heart even when I do not think about it at all. That is the intended destination of the promise that comes from God's mouth. If I have God's Word only in my mind, then my mind will often be busy with other things and I will sin against God. Therefore, it is never sufficient simply to have read God's Word. It must penetrate deep within us, dwell in us, like the Holy of Holies in the Sanctuary, so that we do not sin in thought, word, or deed. It is often better to read a little in the Scriptures and slowly, waiting until it has penetrated within us, than to know a great deal of God's Word but not to treasure it in our hearts.

12 Blessed are you, O LORD;
       instruct me in your statutes.

Do we praise the holiness and piety of human beings
here? Are we concerned with ourselves and our own
purity? Does the "I," which is so noticeably repeated
in these psalm verses, signify preoccupation with the
self in self-criticism and self-justification? Blessed are
you, O Lord! May God alone be blest, who has made
the new beginning with us, who has revealed his Word
to us, who allows himself to be sought and served by
us, who lets his Word dwell within us and protects us
from sin. On the way of the faithful, there is praise
only for God. All their strength and confidence reside
in this praise for God. However, we must ask God
again and again, like beggars: "Instruct me in your
statutes!" (Job 23:12). In blessing God, we confess
what we have received. In making our request of God,
we confess our poverty. Never, as long as we live, will
the request for enlightenment, knowledge, and
growth in understanding of the Word come to an end;
but the praise of him who has given us by his grace
enough and more than enough will never come to an
end in this life or in the life to come.

13 With my lips will I recite
       all the judgments of your mouth.

The judgments of God go forth from his mouth and
should come upon my lips. It is often easy to carry
God's Word in our heart, but very difficult to bring it
upon our lips! Of course, we are not concerned here
with empty lip-service, but with bringing to expression that which fills our heart. Do we not often find
our mouth closed in the presence of great sorrow

because we fear to put a pious formula in place of the divine Word? Is there not an atmosphere of frivolity and godlessness in which we no longer find the right word and simply become silent? Does not false modesty and fear of others often keep our mouths shut? The warning and exhortation remain unspoken, words of comfort and encouragement are denied the one who needs them. In what a tortured and anxious way does the name of Jesus Christ sometimes cross our lips! It requires a great deal of spiritual experience and practice, and at the same time a child-like faith and confidence, to be able to recite with one's lips "all the judgments" of God; and to do so without becoming a spiritual "old hand," a moralizing apostle, an endless prattler. Our whole heart must belong to the Word of God before we learn to place our lips, too, entirely in the service of Jesus Christ.

14 I have taken greater delight in the way
    of your decrees
  than in all manner of riches.

"Delight" is the great word, without which there can be no walking in the way of God. In Matthew we read about the man who found the treasure buried in the field. In his delight he went and sold all that he had and bought that field (Mt. 13:44). All riches and possessions were of no account to him compared to the divine treasure. Yes, in it he found all the riches he could desire.

The one who finds the way of God must first lose all his own riches in order to find in God all manner of riches. God's word creates joy and delight in the one who receives it. It is delight about restored fellowship with God. It is delight about deliverance from fear and sin. It is the joy of the one who had gone astray and, after a long night, has found the right way again. God prepares festive delight for us. He is himself the source of all joy and delight. Yes, he himself knows joy: "As the bridegroom rejoices over the bride, so shall your God rejoice over you" (Is. 62:5). "He will rejoice over you with gladness, he will renew you in his love; he will exult over you with loud singing as on a day of festival" (Zeph. 3:17).

We are invited to participate in this festival in which God delights in the deliverance and the faith of his people. God's Word itself is full of this joy which ought to break forth in us. There is the great proclamation of joy about the incarnation of the Word of God in Jesus Christ in Luke—"Behold, I bring you good news of a great joy which will come to all the people" (Lk. 2:10). The days of our Lord on earth were like the dawning of a single marriage day (Mk. 2:19, cf. Lk. 19:6). There is joy in heaven over the repentance and salvation of each sinner (Lk. 15:7,10). The resurrection and ascension of the Lord fill the disciples with joy (Mt. 28:8; Lk. 24:41,52; Jn. 20:20), and the early church received the communion of Jesus with joyful hearts (Acts 2:46f.). Where the Word of God is, there is joy. As Jesus left the disciples to go to the Father, he said to them: "These things I have spoken to you, that my joy may be in you, and that your joy may be full" (Jn. 15:11). The Word of God brings fullness of joy to its hearers. God intends joy for us; of course, it is a joy "with trembling" (Ps. 2:11) just because it is joy before the holy God. God's Word is the source of all joy, and the way of his decrees is full of delight, because it is the way that God himself has gone and goes with us. Where God is with us, there is joy, and this joy no one will take away from us (Jn. 16:22). In days of affliction and persecution, however, this joy attaches to the promise made by him who has gone before us: "Blessed are you when men revile you and persecute you and utter all kinds of evil against you falsely on my account. Rejoice and be glad, for your reward is great in heaven" (Mt. 5:11f.). These are the riches of the one who follows Jesus.

But the one who will not or cannot go on the way of God knows sadness instead of joy (Mt. 19:22; 17:23). "But I fear that we will have neither the joy nor the cross as long as we accept the gospel so little. We remain as in our old nature, despising the precious treasure of the gospel" (Luther).

15 I will meditate on your commandments
     and give attention to your ways.

There is no standing still. Every gift we receive, every new understanding, drives us still deeper into the Word of God. We need time for God's Word. In order to understand the commandments of God correctly we must meditate at length upon his Word. Nothing could be more wrong than that activism or that feeling of contentment that denies the worth of reflection and meditation. And this is true not just for those who are especially called to it, but for each one who wants to walk in God's ways. Certainly, God will often require quick action; but he also requires stillness and reflection. So we must often remain for hours and days with one and the same word, until we have been enlightened with the right understanding.

No one is so far advanced that she does not need this anymore. No one may think she is dispensed from this because of more urgent demands upon her time. The Word of God demands our time. God himself entered into time and wants us now to give him our time. To be a Christian is not a matter of a moment; it takes time. God gave us the Scripture from which we are to learn his will. Scripture is to be read and considered anew each day. God's Word is not a collection of eternally valid general principles that we can have at our disposal any time we wish. It is the Word of God that is new every day for us in the endless riches of its interpretation. Meditation (that is, prayerful consideration of Scripture) and interpretation are both essential to anyone who seeks God's commandments and not just her own thoughts. A theologian who does not practice both betrays her office. The necessary time for this will be given to every Christian if she really looks for it. Meditation means prayerfully opening our hearts to the Word of God. Interpretation means perceiving and understanding what we find written in Scripture as the Word of God. Each requires the other. Both together constitute that reflection which should be practiced daily.

If I want to know God's commandments, then I should not give attention to myself and my situation, but only to God's ways. What God has done for me in his dealings with his people and in Jesus Christ, what the incarnation, cross, and resurrection of Jesus Christ mean as God's acts for me—that alone should determine my way. "You were bought with a price. So glorify God in your body" (1 Cor. 6:20). "You were bought with a price; do not become slaves of men" (1 Cor. 7:23).

16　My delight is in your statutes;
　　I will not forget your word.

Why is it that my thoughts depart so quickly from God's Word and I find the necessary word is often not there for me in the hour of need? Do I forget to eat and drink and sleep? Why do I forget God's Word? Because I am not yet able to say with the psalmist: "My delight is in your statutes." I never forget that in which I delight. To forget or not is a matter not only of the mind but of the whole person, including the heart. That on which my life and soul depend I cannot forget. The more I begin to love the ordinances of God in creation and in his Word, the more they will be present for me at every hour. Only love guards against forgetting.

Because God's Word was spoken to us in history, in the past, it is necessary for us to repeat what we have learned every day in order to remember it. We must return every day to the saving acts of God in order to be able to go forward. Therefore, Scripture warns us in great earnestness not to forget! "Forget not all his benefits" (Ps. 103:2). "Take heed lest you forget the LORD, who brought you out of the land of Egypt, out of the house of bondage" (Deut. 6:12—read the whole chapter!). "Remember Jesus Christ" (2 Tim. 2:8). Faith and obedience live by our remembering and repeating. Remembering becomes a power in the present because the God who once acted for me is the living God who today makes me sure of what he has done. The past in itself is indifferent. But because in the past something decisive happened *for me,* that which was past becomes present when I grasp the "for me" in faith; "for the word 'for me' requires only believing hearts" (Luther).

Because my salvation lies not in me but outside myself, because my righteousness is the righteousness of Jesus Christ alone, because that can only be proclaimed to me in the Word, remembering and repeating are necessary for blessedness, and forgetting is equivalent to falling away from the faith.

In my daily remembering of Jesus Christ, I receive the promise that God loved me from eternity and has not forgotten me (Is. 49:14ff.). Knowing that God does not forget me because he loves me, I experience delight and am filled with love for God's faithfulness revealed in his Word. So I learn to say: "I will not forget your word."

17 Deal bountifully with your servant,
        that I may live and keep your word.

I ask to live the way a servant asks his master. Life is a good gift from God. Life is not a means to an end, but it is in itself fulfillment. God created us that we might live, he reconciled and saved us that we might live. He does not want to see ideas triumph over a pile of corpses. Ideas exist for the sake of life, not life for the sake of ideas. Where life itself is made into an idea, real life (created and redeemed life) is more thoroughly destroyed than by any other idea. Life is God's purpose for us. If it becomes a means to an end, then a contradiction is introduced that makes life a torment. Then the goal, that which is considered to be good, is sought beyond life and can only be obtained by the denial of life. That was the condition in which we found ourselves before we received life in God, and we had been taught to call that condition good. We were haters and despisers of life, and lovers and worshipers of ideas.

I ask God for the good gift of life, knowing that only the life that he gives is a good gift. All other life is torment. Only the life from God is purposeful and fulfilling, overcoming the contradiction between what is and what ought to be. Life is a time of grace, death is judgment. Therefore, life is a gift from God's bounty, because I am given time for the grace of God. Such time is mine as long as the Word of God is with me. To hold fast to this Word is the affirmation of life from God. God's Word is not beyond this life; it does not diminish life by making it a means to an end; rather, it protects life from contradiction and from the rule of ideas. God's Word is the fulfillment of life, beyond which there is no further goal. Therefore, I ask God for the bountiful gift of life, which belongs to him, as the life of a servant belongs to the master—the life that will be fulfilled through keeping the Word of God.

18 Open my eyes, that I may see
the wonders of your law.

I must close the eyes of sense if I want to see what God shows me. God first makes me blind when he wants to let me see his Word. Then he opens my blind eyes, and I see what otherwise I could never have recognized, that God's law is full of wonders. How could I go through the length of this psalm and begin it ever anew, how should I not grow weary of this incessant repetition, if God did not enable me to see that each of

his words is full of undiscovered, unfathomable wonder? How should I keep to God's Word daily without
eyes that have been opened so that they want to look
their fill into the depth and glory of this Word?

To the eyes of my reason, God's law appears to be a
perhaps necessary but soon-learned rule of life, about
which there is not much more to think, to say, or to be
amazed at. As long as I intend to see with these eyes, I
will have no desire that my eyes be opened. But if I
have become blind, if God has led me into the depth
of night, if I am covered by the darkness of my need
and guilt so that my natural eyes are able to perceive
nothing more, then I will cry out for the better light to
see by. Only one who is blind cries out that his eyes
may be opened. But is this psalmist, who so highly values God's Word, a blind person? It is, in fact, the one
who has glanced at the wonders of God's law who
knows how blind he still is and how much he needs
his eyes to be opened in order not to sink back into
total darkness. We pray anew every day, when we open
our eyes in the morning and when we close them at
night, that God will enlighten the eyes of the heart, to
remain open when our natural vision is deceived in
the daylight and when the night puts before us mere
dreams. We pray that God will give us enlightened
eyes, which are always filled with the wonders of his
law.

We must do as blind Bartimaeus did when he heard
that Jesus was going past him on the Jericho Road. He
allowed no one to silence him, but cried out for help
until Jesus heard him. To the question of Jesus: "What
do you want me to do for you?" he answered: "Master,
let me receive my sight." And so he was healed (Mk.

10:46ff.). But, as it was with the blind man of Bethsaida (Mk. 8:22f.), who only gained his sight gradually and in stages, so also our eyes will only slowly be opened and will proceed from one perception to the next.

But whoever thinks that he can see when he is, in fact, blind can no longer be helped; he will perish in his blindness (Jn. 9:40f.). It is a gift of grace to be able to recognize one's blindness with respect to God's Word and to be able to pray with opened eyes.

The one whose eyes have been opened by God for his Word looks into a world of wonders. What appeared to me to be dead is full of life, what was contradictory resolves itself in a higher unity, harsh requirements become gracious commands. In the midst of human words I hear God's eternal Word, in past history I recognize the saving acts of the God who is present for me now. God lays claim to me through words of comfort, and the unbearable burden becomes an easy yoke. The great wonder in the law of God is the revelation of the Lord Jesus Christ. Through him what is written comes alive, contradictions are resolved, and the revelation is given its unfathomable depth. Lord, open my eyes.

19 I am a stranger here on earth;
do not hide your commandments from me.
When God's Word found me for the first time, it made me a stranger on this earth. It placed me in the long succession of the forebears of the faith, who lived as aliens in the promised land (Heb. 11:9). Abraham believed the call that bade him go from his own land into the land of promise; yet, in his old age, after

Sarah's death, he received as a "stranger and a sojourner" ground enough for a burial place as his only possession in the promised land (Gen. 23:4). Jacob confessed to Pharaoh that his entire life had been a pilgrimage, briefer and harder still than the pilgrimages of his fathers Isaac and Abraham (Gen. 47:9). When the children of Israel took firm possession of the land of Canaan, they were never allowed to forget that they had been strangers, too, and that they still were. They had been strangers in Egypt (Ex. 22:20), and they remained to that day "strangers and sojourners" in the land that did not belong to them but to God (Lev. 25:23). In a great and festive hour of his life, David included himself with these ancestors, when he said: "For we are strangers before thee, and sojourners, as all our fathers were; our days on the earth are like a shadow, and there is no abiding" (1 Chron. 29:15).

I am a stranger on earth. Therefore, I confess that I cannot remain here, that my given time is brief. Nor do I have any claim here to houses and possessions. The good things that I enjoy I must thankfully receive, but I must also endure injustice and violence with no one to intercede for me. I have no firm hold on either persons or things. As a stranger, I am subject to the laws of the place where I sojourn. The earth, which nourishes me, has a right to my work and my strength. I have no right to despise the earth on which I live. I owe it loyalty and gratitude. It is my lot to be a stranger and a sojourner, but this cannot become a reason for evading God's call so that I dream away my earthly life with thoughts of heaven.

There is a very godless homesickness for the other world that is not consistent with really finding one's home there. I ought to behave myself like a guest here, with all that entails. I should not stay aloof and refuse to participate in the tasks, joys, and sorrows of earth, while I am waiting patiently for the redemption of the divine promise. I am really to wait for the promise and not try to steal it in advance in wishes and dreams. Nothing is said here at all about the homeland itself. I know that it cannot be this earth, and yet I know that the earth is God's and that I am on this earth not only as its guest but as God's wayfarer and sojourner (Ps. 39:14). However, since I am on earth only as a stranger and guest, without rights, without permanent residence, without security, the very God who made me this weak and insignificant has given me one firm pledge for my goal: his Word. This one thing that is certain he will not take away from me; he will keep his Word for me, and in it he will let me sense his power. Where the Word is at home with me, I am able to find my way in the strange land—to find what is right where there is injustice, a place to stand where there is uncertainty, strength for my work, and patience in time of sorrow.

"Do not hide your commandments from me." That is the prayer of the pilgrim in a strange land.

For those who have become strangers on earth, according to God's will and his calling, there is really only one thought that can fill them with dread—that they might no longer recognize God's will, no longer know what God requires of them. Indeed, God is often hidden in the course of our personal lives or in his action in history; but that is not what causes us anguish. No, it is the fear that the revealed commandment of God might be obscured, so that we no longer know from God's Word what we are to do. In the midst of our happy certainty of the commandments of God, this fear overtakes us: What if God should hide his commandments from me one day? I would collapse into nothing; I would stumble and fall at my first step in the strange land.

But now I must ask myself whether I am already guided so much by my own principles that I might not even notice if God withdrew his living commandment from me one day. I might go on acting in accordance with my principles, but God's commandment would no longer be with me. God's commandment is God's personal word to me for this present day, for my day-to-day living. Of course, God's commandment is not today this and tomorrow that, since God's law is at one with itself. But it makes all the difference whether I obey God or my principles. If I am content with my principles, then I cannot understand the prayer of the psalmist. But if I allow myself to be shown the way by God, then I will depend entirely on the grace that is revealed or denied to me; then I will tremble as I receive each word from the mouth of God, because of my need for the next word and for his continuing grace. Thus I will remain in all my ways and my decisions totally bound to grace, and no false security will be able to lure me away from this living fellowship with God.

"Do not hide your commandments from me" is a cry that comes only from the heart of one who knows God's commandments. There can be no doubt that God has given us his commandments to know; we cannot plead that we did not know the will of God. God does not allow us to live with unresolvable conflicts, nor does he turn our lives into moral tragedies. He gives us his will to know; he requires its fulfillment and punishes the disobedient. Things are much simpler here than we would prefer. It is not that we do not know God's commandments, but that we do not keep them. And then, of course, as a result of such disobedience, we also gradually stop recognizing them. That is our situation. It is not stated here that God does hide his commandments; rather, God is appealed to, that by his grace he will not hide them. It stands within God's freedom and wisdom to withdraw from us the grace of his commandments; but that should not produce resignation in us. Instead, we should all the more join in the urgent and incessant prayer: Do not hide your commandments from me.

20 My soul is consumed at all times
    with longing for your judgments.

The longing for God's judgments is more powerful than the soul. The soul is consumed when the God-given longing for his Word comes over it. This longing to know God's judgments, cost what it may, is not a power of the soul; on the contrary, it is the soul's death. No longer the soul, but the single longing for God's Word lives in me and brings to silence all my many other wishes and inclinations. My soul cannot prevent every thought and every moment from being filled with it. In order to see, to acknowledge, to understand God's right and God's requirements over against all human claims, the soul must offer everything in sacrifice. When this longing for God comes over us, then the soul suffers torment, then it is prostrate, then its fine structure is consumed. Whoever makes her pilgrimage to the promised land does not concern herself about the dust, sweat, and wounds that cover her; she is concerned only about the goal.

Because the longing for God's Word is not born of the soul, it does not pass away in an hour or a day like a movement or stirring of the soul. It is not to be compared to the longing of the soul for a dear friend; this lasts only for a time, while the longing for God that consumes the soul is for "all times." It could not be otherwise, for it comes upon us from God himself and so must be everlasting. It has virtually nothing to do with a sudden welling-up or momentary giving of the heart to God's Word. It is distinguished from that by being there "at all times." It is not the warmth of pious feeling but endurance in the Word unto the end that characterizes this longing for God's Word.

For this reason it would be false to confuse this longing with the soul's exalted religious feelings. On the contrary, it is the experience of the soul's being consumed and destroyed by this longing that is spoken of here. It does not consist in the bliss of religious rapture. It consists in our being able to hope and rely upon God's cause even when we see the triumph of the arrogant cause of human beings, in our not being able to forget the homeland though we live in a strange country, in knowing that we cannot break from God's grasp even in our misery, need, and guilt, in being compelled to seek him where reason and experience deny him, in knowing God's Word as a power over our life that never lets us go, though all our powers sink into death. Understood in this way, "at all times" is no exaggeration but a reality.

21 You have rebuked the insolent;
　　cursed are they who stray from your
　　commandments!

God hates the insolent, those who are content with themselves, who care nothing for justice and mercy, who despise the Word of God and the faithful. Pride before God is the root of all disobedience, all violence, all irresponsibility. Pride is the root of all rebellion and destruction. Confronting all pride and insolence, however, is a fearful warning, of which the proud themselves comprehend nothing, but the faithful do; it is the gospel. "God opposes the proud, but gives grace to the humble" (1 Peter 5:5). The cross of Jesus Christ, which shows that God is with the weak and the humble, is God's rebuke to the insolent. They may achieve victory over all human beings, but against God they will come to nought.

Whoever believes in the gospel sees the Word of God hanging over the insolent of this earth. The preaching of the Word of God is the only serious rebuke to a humanity grown proud. But, along with his Word, God has also given signs of his might. In the midst of history, here and there, God's rebuke can be seen, and the community of the faithful look with shuddering and amazement at the proud, who even now in their time fall and are destroyed. They are kept from any hypocritical certainty, however, because they see that innocent people are always destroyed along with the proud; and so the visible judgments of God remain hidden and obscure even for the faithful. Only the Word remains incontrovertibly clear when it pronounces its curse on the godless: "Cursed are they who stray from your commandments!" In the law it says:

"Cursed be he who does not confirm the words of this law by doing them" (Deut. 27:26). Can we speak this word without being convicted by it ourselves? Is it a word only for others and not for ourselves? The curse upon the transgressors of the law of God is God's right and....

(Here the manuscript breaks off.)

22 Turn from me shame and rebuke,
   for I have kept your decrees.
23 Even though rulers sit and plot against me,
   I will meditate on your statutes.
24 For your decrees are my delight,
   and they are my counselors.

DIETRICH BONHOEFFER
FEBRUARY 4, 1906—APRIL 9, 1945

NOTES

1. Dietrich Bonhoeffer, *Fiction from Prison,* ed. Renate and Eberhard Bethge, trans. Ursula Hoffman (Philadelphia, 1981), 61. *Fragmente aus Tegel. Drama und Roman* (Munich, 1978), 80-81. (My translation.)

2. *Dietrich Bonhoeffer: Memories and Perspectives,* PBS documentary, available for rental from the Episcopal Media Center, Atlanta, Georgia.

3. Eberhard Bethge, *Dietrich Bonhoeffer: Man of Vision, Man of Courage,* trans. Mosbacher, Ross, *et al.* (New York, 1970), 512.

4. Ibid.

5. Dietrich Bonhoeffer, *Gesammelte Schriften,* ed. Eberhard Bethge (Chr. Kaiser Verlag, Munich), VI: 521; IV:257; IV:258. (Henceforth, GS.) Quoted in Herbert Pelikan, *Die Frommigkeit Dietrich Bonhoeffers* (Vienna, 1982), 57, 64.

6. Dietrich Bonhoeffer, *Psalms: The Prayer Book of the Bible,* trans. James H. Burtness (Minneapolis, 1974), 32-33. (My translation from GS: IV:555.)

7. Ibid., 11-12. (GS: IV:545.)

8. *Begegnungen mit Dietrich Bonhoeffer: Ein Almanach,* ed. Wolf-Dieter Zimmermann (Munich, 1964), 120.

9. Bethge, *Dietrich Bonhoeffer*, 571.

10. Ibid., 580.

11. Dietrich Bonhoeffer, *Life Together*, trans. John W. Doberstein (New York, 1954); originally published as *Gemeinsames Leben* (Munich, 1939), 46.

12. Ibid., 47.

13. Bonhoeffer, *Psalms*, 31-32.

14. GS IV:597f. An English translation of this meditation by John D. Godsey can be found in his *Preface to Bonhoeffer: The Man and Two of His Shorter Writings* (Philadelphia, 1965).

15. Bethge, *Dietrich Bonhoeffer*, 335, 571.

16. Richard Meux Benson, *The War Songs of the Prince of Peace* (London, 1901), I:10; Richard Meux Benson, *The Religious Vocation* (London, 1939), 183.

17. Richard Meux Benson, *The Way of Holiness* (London, 1901), 2.

18. GS II:478-482. For the biographical information, see Bethge, *Dietrich Bonhoeffer*, 381-383, and for the letter to Karl Barth, GS II:284f.

19. GS IV:290-293; Bethge, *Dietrich Bonhoeffer*, 388.

20. GS III:26-31.

21. GS II:583-585; see Bethge, *Dietrich Bonhoeffer*, 656.

22. GS V:434-439; see Bethge, *Dietrich Bonhoeffer*, 79.

23. GS IV:391-399; see Bethge, *Dietrich Bonhoeffer*, 13.

24. GS IV:223-224; Bethge, *Dietrich Bonhoeffer*, 413, 344.

25. GS IV:456-460; see Bethge, *Dietrich Bonhoeffer*, 201, 420.

26. GS IV:413-422; see Bethge, *Dietrich Bonhoeffer*, 483-489.

27. GS IV:595-596. See Bethge, *Dietrich Bonhoeffer*, 703ff; also 554, 560, 565.

28. GS IV:505-543. See Bethge, *Dietrich Bonhoeffer*, 497; also 388-389.

COWLEY PUBLICATIONS is a ministry of the Society of St. John the Evangelist, a religious community for men in the Episcopal Church. Emerging from the Society's tradition of prayer, theological reflection, and diversity of mission, the press is centered in the rich heritage of the Anglican Communion.

Cowley Publications seeks to provide books, audio cassettes, and other resources for the ongoing theological exploration and spiritual development of the Episcopal Church and others in the body of Christ. To this end, it is dedicated to developing a new generation of theological writers, encouraging them to produce timely, creative, and stimulating publications of excellence, and making these publications available widely, reaching both clergy and lay persons.